RELATION OF SCI-TECH INFORMATION TO ENVIRONMENTAL STUDIES

Edited by
ELLIS MOUNT

LONDON AND NEW YORK

First published in 1990 by The Haworth Press, Inc.

This edition first published in 2020
by Routledge
2 Park Square, Milton Park, Abingdon, Oxon OX14 4RN

and by Routledge
52 Vanderbilt Avenue, New York, NY 10017

Routledge is an imprint of the Taylor & Francis Group, an informa business

© 1990 The Haworth Press, Inc.

All rights reserved. No part of this book may be reprinted or reproduced or utilised in any form or by any electronic, mechanical, or other means, now known or hereafter invented, including photocopying and recording, or in any information storage or retrieval system, without permission in writing from the publishers.

Trademark notice: Product or corporate names may be trademarks or registered trademarks, and are used only for identification and explanation without intent to infringe.

British Library Cataloguing in Publication Data
A catalogue record for this book is available from the British Library

ISBN: 978-0-367-34616-4 (Set)
ISBN: 978-0-429-34352-0 (Set) (ebk)
ISBN: 978-0-367-36407-6 (Volume 77) (hbk)
ISBN: 978-0-367-36409-0 (Volume 77) (pbk)
ISBN: 978-0-429-34570-8 (Volume 77) (ebk)

Publisher's Note
The publisher has gone to great lengths to ensure the quality of this reprint but points out that some imperfections in the original copies may be apparent.

Disclaimer
The publisher has made every effort to trace copyright holders and would welcome correspondence from those they have been unable to trace.

Relation of Sci-Tech Information to Environmental Studies

Ellis Mount
Editor

The Haworth Press
New York • London

Relation of Sci-Tech Information to Environmental Studies has also been published as *Science & Technology Libraries*, Volume 10, Number 2, Winter 1989.

© 1990 by The Haworth Press, Inc. All rights reserved. No part of this book may be reproduced or utilized in any form or by any means, electronic or mechanical, including photocopying, microfilm and recording, or by any information storage and retrieval system, without permission in writing from the publisher. Printed in the United States of America.

The Haworth Press, Inc., 10 Alice Street, Binghamton, NY 13904-1580
EUROSPAN/Haworth, 3 Henrietta Street, London WC2E 8LU England

Library of Congress Cataloging-in-Publication Data

Relation of sci-tech information to environmental studies / Ellis Mount, editor.
   p. cm.
   "Has also been published as Science & technology libraries, volume 10, number 2, 1989."
   ISBN 0-86656-988-X : $24.95
   1. Environmental libraries. 2. Environmental protection—Information services. 3. Environmental protection—Research—Methodology. I. Mount, Ellis.
Z675.E75R45   1990
026.5—dc20   89-71657
                                                                                               CIP

Relation of Sci-Tech Information to Environmental Studies

CONTENTS

Introduction	1
Technology Transfer and the U.S. Environmental Protection Agency's Library Network *Monique C. Currie* *Barbara S. Roth*	3
Technology Transfer and the EPA Library Network	3
EPA Library Network	4
Special Collections	6
Specialized Libraries	7
Data Sharing	9
Technology	11
Expertise and Knowledge to Share	12
EPA Network Libraries	14
The Center for Environmental Information: Meeting Community Information Needs *Frederick W. Stoss*	17
Introduction	17
Founding and Early History	18
Going International with Acid Rain	20
CEI Organization	23
What Lies Ahead	27
Environmental Publications of the American Chemical Society *Maureen Welling Matkovich*	29
Introduction	29
Formal Publications	30

Environmental Information for Wider Distribution	33
Divisional Publications	36
Conclusion	37

Adirondack Research Center: Research Resource on the Adirondacks   39
   Maryde F. King

I. Adirondack Research Center Background	39
II. Adirondack Research Center Collection	40
III. Research Use of the Collection	42
IV. Cooperation with Other Research and Educational Groups	43

Current Awareness Objective of Reference Serial Focusing on Environmental Issues: A Look at *Environmental Periodicals Bibliography*   47
   Joanne St. John

Outgrowth of Environmental Crisis	47
Focus on Accessibility of Information	49
Additional Service	54
Gearing Up for Special Interest Publications	56

Bowker A & I Environment Database: Major Features and Editorial Policies   57
   David J. Packer

SPECIAL PAPER

Computer Searching of Chemical Databases by Faculty and Students at the University of Rochester   67
   Arleen N. Somerville

Introduction	67
Promotion	68
Objectives	70
Teaching Techniques	71

Teaching Chemical Abstracts	73
Teaching Substructure Searching	83
Logistics	89
Costs	91
Liaison Activities	91
Search Frequency	92
Staying Current	93
Impact of Program	93
Future	94

SCI-TECH COLLECTIONS 99
Tony Stankus, Editor

The Search for Psychological Well-Being in Captive Nonhuman Primates: Information Sources 101
Andrew J. Petto
Melinda A. Novak
Sydney Ann Fingold
Arlene C. Walsh

Introduction	102
Psychological Well-Being in Captive Primates	103
Search Strategies	104
Successful Searching	105
Defining Psychological Well-Being	108
Identifying and Measuring Psychological Well-Being	109
Interpreting and Implementing Programs and Policies	109
Interacting with a Concerned Public	110
Conclusions	111

NEW REFERENCE WORKS IN SCIENCE AND TECHNOLOGY 129
Arleen N. Somerville, Editor

SCI-TECH ONLINE   **145**
   Ellen Nagle, Editor

Tenth National Online Meeting   145
Database News   146
Publications and Search Aids   148

SCI-TECH IN REVIEW   **151**
   Karla Pearce, Editor

Introduction

No one needs to be reminded that the world faces serious environmental problems, ranging from uncertain purity of water supplies in many communities to the more global problem of acid rain, to name but two examples. What many people may not have realized is the close relationship of scientific and technical research and engineering projects to the search for a solution to each environmental dilemma. Behind such research and active projects is the large body of sci-tech information, found in libraries and information centers around the world.

The purpose of this volume is to present articles which show the nature and the use of sci-tech information in relaton to environmental problems. It includes the efforts of several disciplines, such as sci-tech librarians, government researchers, compilers and/or editors of noted indexing/abstracting services.

The first paper is from the U.S. Environmental Protection Agency, written by Monique C. Currie and Barbara S. Roth. It describes the EPA library network of some 25 libraries located throughout the country. Services offered by the network and their collections are also discussed. Another environmental organization, the Center for Environmental Information, Inc., is the subject of the next paper, written by Frederick W. Stoss. He reviews the growth of this non-profit, non-advocacy organization and comments on its programs, such as establishing the Acid Rain Information Clearinghouse, as well as its library.

The relationship of the American Chemical Society's publications to environmental matters is discussed in the paper by Maureen Welling Matkovich. She shows the range of its output to include journals, books, newsletters, meeting abstracts and publications for wider distribution. Following this is the paper by Maryde F. King, who has written on the growth of the Adirondack Research Center, including the use made of its library collection in furthering the

© 1990 by The Haworth Press, Inc. All rights reserved.

efforts of researchers to study conservation topics as they relate to this important area.

The next two papers deal with commercial publications, the first dealing with *Environmental Periodicals Bibliography* in a paper written by Joanne St. John. She describes the main features of this bibliography, now available in both printed and online formats. The other paper, written by David J. Packer, describes the development and operation of one of the Bowker A & I databases, namely Environment Database, which was acquired in 1988 by the R. R. Bowker Company. He discusses the three retrieval formats available — a monthly abstract journal, a hardbound annual cumulation and an online database.

The special paper for this volume presents a review of the program for instructing students and faculty members at the University of Rochester in online searching of chemical databases. The author, Arleen N. Somerville, traces the growth of the program along with a discussion of its promotion, teaching techniques and impact.

This volume's collection development paper has to do with research on the psychological well-being of nonhuman primates, a difficult area related to recent legislation and social pressures. It was written by Andrew J. Petto, Melinda A. Novak, Sydney Ann Fingold and Arlene C. Walsh.

Our contributed sections dealing with available reference works, with developments in online searching and with recent publications relating to sci-tech libraries complete the volume.

Ellis Mount
Editor

Technology Transfer and the U.S. Environmental Protection Agency's Library Network

Monique C. Currie
Barbara S. Roth

SUMMARY. The library network of the U.S. Environmental Protection Agency is composed of a Headquarters library, ten Regional libraries and fifteen specialized or scientific libraries located throughout the country. Technology transfer may be defined as "the use of technical knowledge in an area other than the one for which the research and development was originally performed." This article reviews the contributions of the network libraries and librarians to the Agency's technology transfer efforts. In doing so it highlights many of the special and unique collections and services of the network libraries.

TECHNOLOGY TRANSFER AND THE EPA LIBRARY NETWORK

As the programs of the U.S. Environmental Protection Agency expand and evolve, more of the work in environmental protection is being carried out by EPA Regional offices, State and local government agencies. Additionally, major environmental legislation such as the Clean Air Act, the Clean Water Act, the Resource Conserva-

---

Monique C. Currie is Reference Librarian with Labat-Anderson, Inc., under contract to the Headquarters Library of the U.S. Environmental Protection Agency, Washington, DC, 20460. She received her BA (Geography) from the University of Wisconsin, Madison and her MLIS from the University of California, Berkeley. Barbara S. Roth is the former Chief of the Information Services Branch, U.S. Environmental Protection Agency and is now with the Agency's Office of Solid Waste, Washington, DC, 20460. She received her BA (Political Science) from American University and her MA from the University of Illinois in Urban Planning.

© 1990 by The Haworth Press, Inc. All rights reserved.

tion and Recovery Act, Superfund, the Safe Drinking Water Act and the Clean Water Act, all mandate more involvement by State and local government. This has had a significant impact on EPA's approach to carrying out its mission, prompting the Agency to extend its role beyond a traditional focus on enforcement and regulation to a renewed emphasis on technology transfer and training as a means of accomplishing its goals.[1]

Technology transfer can be defined as "the use of technical knowledge in an area other than the one for which the research and development was originally performed."[2] The technology which is transferred can be ideas and techniques, computer applications, management tools, products or expertise. The transfer can be accomplished in a variety of ways including: joint development projects, continuing professional education, consulting arrangements, clearinghouses and information centers or libraries.

One vehicle the U.S. Environmental Protection Agency (EPA) utilizes to achieve this goal is the EPA library network.

EPA LIBRARY NETWORK

The Environmental Protection Agency Network is composed of a Headquarters Office in Washington, DC, ten Regional offices and fifteen specialized, scientific laboratories located throughout the country. The libraries contain a combined collection of over 127,538 books, 355,917 reports, 5,048 journals, 2,998,513 microform documents, 9,000 journal article reprints and 2,000 maps.

The libraries offer a variety of products and services to EPA staff, contractors, State and local governments and the general public. Such services include:

REFERENCE—Assistance with your research questions by either finding the answers or assisting you in locating sources of information within the library's collection.

REFERRALS—Directing you to sources of information outside of the EPA Network.

INTERLIBRARY LOAN—Maintenance of cooperative agreements which enable academic, public, and specialized libraries to borrow books and journals from EPA libraries.

PUBLICATIONS — Production of useful bibliographies and finding guides.

DATABASE SEARCHING — EPA libraries have access to online versions of hundreds of technical and environmental indexes/abstracts including Enviroline, Pollution Abstracts and Public Affairs Information Service and can produce customized lists of relevant citations. Searches are done free for EPA staff and registered contractors. Searching is done on a limited basis for States and the public. Whenever possible, library staff will direct States and the public to no-cost EPA databases or vendors of commercial databases. The library network's catalog of holdings is also available online. (See Figure 1 [EPA Library Network].)

FIGURE 1

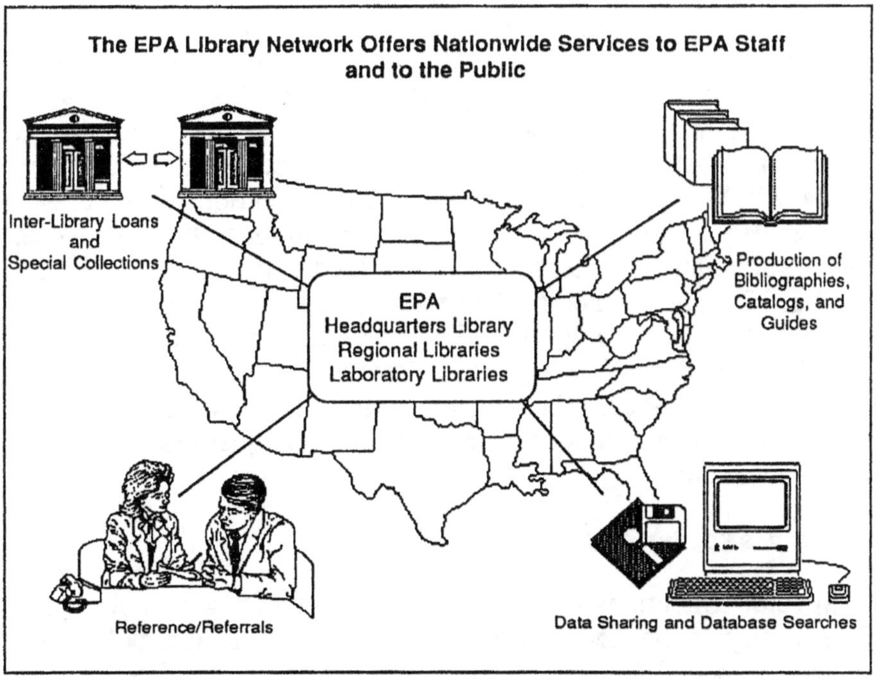

The EPA Library Network Offers Nationwide Services to EPA Staff and to the Public

- Inter-Library Loans and Special Collections
- EPA Headquarters Library, Regional Libraries, Laboratory Libraries
- Production of Bibliographies, Catalogs, and Guides
- Reference/Referrals
- Data Sharing and Database Searches

Originally appeared in *Cooperative Environmental Message*, January 9, 1989, published by USEPA Technology Transfer Staff, Washington, DC. Publication #EPA-009.

SPECIAL COLLECTIONS

Many of the Regional and laboratory libraries have established special collections within their libraries. These "collections within collections" are generally organized around a single environmental topic and are physically separated from the rest of the library's collection. Special collections are popular with EPA staff because they help centralize materials in a single place. It also serves as a referral for members of the public searching topical information. Librarians coordinate the development of special collections with the particular regulations or research and development activities of their laboratories or Regions. The following are examples of special collections in the EPA library network.

Hazardous Waste Collection

To support the information needs in the Superfund offices of the Agency, the Hazardous Waste Collection was established in 1986. The collection contains EPA reports, commercial books, policy and guidance directives, legislation and regulations on the subject of hazardous waste. The main collection is housed in the Headquarters Library in Washington, DC, with satellite collections found in each of the EPA Regional libraries and the laboratory libraries in Ada, OK; Cincinnati, OH; Edison, NJ; Research Triangle Park, NC; Las Vegas, NV; and the National Enforcement Investigations Center in Denver, CO. A bibliographic database which runs on an IBM PC AT/XT with a user friendly menu accompanies the collection, enabling patrons to search the contents by title, keyword, issuing office or date. Contact Monique Currie at the Headquarters Library for more information.

Chesapeake Bay Collection

Special collections can be organized around a geographic area. The library of the Central Regional Laboratory in Annapolis, MD, houses a special Chesapeake Bay Collection. The collection consists of general books, maps and even navigation charts of the Bay. Of particular significance, notes librarian Meg Monro, are a nearly complete collection of Johns Hopkins University and Chesapeake

Research Consortium Reports. Dating back to the early 1960s, these reports record some 30 years of changes in water quality and Bay aquatic life. Users of this unique collection include public interest groups such as the Chesapeake Bay Foundation, scientists from the University of Maryland's Center for Estuarine and Environmental Studies and researchers from the Smithsonian.

Risk Collection in Cincinnati

The newest special collection in the network is the Dr. Jerry F. Stara Risk Assessment Collection at the Andrew W. Briendenbach Environmental Research Center Library (AWBERC) in Cincinnati, OH. Dedicated in June 1988, it contains over 300 books, EPA reports and journals on the subject of risk assessment. The core of the collection is composed of the personal and departmental materials and books of ECAO scientists, among them the late Dr. Stara for whom the collection is named. In recognition of the contributions of Dr. Stara in the risk field, Princeton Scientific, a private publisher of scientific and technical materials has donated a number of new books to the collection. Contact Robert Rettig at AWBERC for more information.

SPECIALIZED LIBRARIES

Looking at the EPA Library Network as a whole, some of the libraries are themselves special collections.

Law Library

Maintained by the EPA's Office of General Counsel in Washington, DC, the Law Library's collection focuses primarily on Federal environmental law. Its unique archival collection includes: *General Counsel Opinions* from 1970 to the present, a complete collection of *Title 40 of the Code of Federal Regulation, Protection of the Environment, Bid Protest Decisions*, and *Assistance Dispute Decisions*. Reference assistance, including the searching of legal databases, is provided to EPA staff throughout the country. Reference and referral service is extended to the public as well, particularly private law firms nationwide.

Office of Toxic Substances
Non-Confidential Information Center

Also known as the OTS Library, this EPA library located in Washington, DC, primarily serves the staff of EPA's Office of Toxic Substances, but the general public is free to use any of the resources within the library, and library staff can provide information to the public concerning the availability of documents produced by the Office of Toxic Substances. It maintains a collection particularly strong in the areas of physical chemistry, toxicology, public health, and biotechnology. Also housed is a unique collection of chemical literature, known as the Chemical Collection System (CCS). It is a collection of over 144,000 journal articles of standard references relating to chemicals studied by the Office of Toxic Substances. Included are obscure, foreign language articles, some even dating back to the early 1900s. The collection is indexed on a database, currently accessed in the OTS Library only. The public can gain access to the articles through interlibrary loan with a complete citation.

National Enforcement Investigation Center
(NEIC) Library

Part of the EPA since 1970, the National Enforcement Investigation Center (NEIC) in Denver, CO, serves as the principal source of expertise involving civil and criminal litigation support for complex investigations having national and/or significant Regional impact on EPA and State regulatory programs for air, water, toxics, pesticides, radiation and solid waste pollution control. The library is an integral part of NEIC, and the focal point for inquiries to the Information Services Section. The library provides automated research, reference, referral and interlibrary loan service to support NEIC's programs. Library services are extended to employees of Federal, State and local government. The NEIC library collection emphasizes environmental law and regulations, chemistry, hazardous waste and environmental auditing. The collection includes a comprehensive repository of EPA consent decrees. Through the cooperation of the Land and Natural Resources Division of the Department of Justice, the consent decree collection is accessible full text on the Justice Retrieval and Inquiry System (JURIS).

DATA SHARING

Libraries have a tradition of sharing information. EPA libraries are open to the public and serve as a convenient and visible reference point to the local community. Efforts already under way to share information include:

Library Bulletins

Regional and laboratory libraries distribute their respective library bulletins announcing newly acquired books and reports to each member of the Regional or laboratory staff. The libraries also send these bulletins to State and local environmental libraries. These lists help to get the word out on newly published EPA reports and informally function as a guide to purchasing commercial environmental books. To receive copies of such bulletins, contact your nearest EPA library.

Network Holdings

The network catalog is a complete listing of all the books, reports, journals, abstract and indexes found in the nationwide network of EPA libraries. Many of the libraries distribute older editions of the EPA Network Library's catalog to local libraries. For example, the Region 9 library sends its microfiche catalog of library holdings to the Water Resources Department Library at the University of California, Los Angeles, and to the Toxic Substance Control Division Library of the Department of Health Services of the State of California in Sacramento. These catalogs help to share the wealth of information available at the Regional libraries with more remote locations.

Directory of State Environmental Libraries

Recently compiled is the *Directory of State Environmental Libraries*, EPA/IMSD/88-010, Oct. 1988. The directory is part of an EPA initiative to expand information sharing between EPA and the States. It contains information on the collections and services provided by State environmental libraries. For more information contact Mary Patterson, Information Services Branch EPA Headquarters (202) 382-5929.

Two-Way Flow of Information

Technology transfer efforts initiated by the EPA Library network have resulted in a two-way transfer of information both in and out of the Federal government. The Region 9 library in San Francisco serves as the repository for exhibits and testimony concerning the San Francisco Estuary/Bay Delta Hearings Project. Members of the general public, concerned citizens groups, State and local officials are able to gain online access through a terminal provided by the State of California's Regional Water Quality Control Board to the full text of the testimony as maintained by the Board. Users are also able to browse the hard copy of the exhibits in the library.

In Seattle, the Region 10 library displayed a week-long exhibit on wetlands as provided by the Department of Ecology of the State of Washington. As a participant in the annual observance of Coastweeks, the Headquarters Library prepared a book display, bibliography of current library materials on oceans and their coasts. Sponsored by an alliance of organizations including the Sierra Club, the League of Women Voters and the Coastal States Organization, Coastweeks is a three-week educational celebration of the resources and beauty of our Nation's coasts.

Such efforts are not limited to exchanges merely between the States and EPA. Peg Nelson, EPA librarian in Region 1, Boston, is a member of the Data Management Workgroup of the Cape Cod Aquifer Management Project (CCAMP). The two-year effort is a cooperative venture between EPA, the Massachusetts Department of Environmental Quality Engineering, the Cape Cod Planning and Economic Development Commission and the U.S. Geological Survey. Its mission is to ensure the protection of Cape Cod. Ms. Nelson identified reports and maps on the subject of Cape Cod authored by those agencies and produced a bibliography of these sources. The bibliography, *CCAMP Bibliographies, Publications and maps*, EPA 901/3-88-002, Sept. 1988, is available to the public and is being distributed to target groups in the Cape Cod area. For more information call Peg Nelson in the Region 1 Library.

Bibliographies

Many of the EPA libraries regularly produce bibliographies on selected environmental topics at the request of EPA program offices. Library staff work with EPA program staff to select citations of current materials on subjects such as radon or indoor air pollution. The result is a well-organized, neutral source of information helpful to be used as a resource when staff answers public requests for environmental information.

TECHNOLOGY

EPA network librarians have been especially adept at using technology itself to further aid their efforts to disseminate information.

Online EPA Library Network Catalog

This electronic version of the EPA library network catalog enables users to browse the entire holding of the EPA network libraries from their desktops. Using a personal computer, modem and communications software, EPA staff and registered State and Federal users can search the catalog through a user-friendly menu with context-sensitive help. Library patrons can locate materials by the traditional author or title identification, but this online version of the catalog greatly expands their searching options to include date, keywords and library location. For more information please contact Brigid Rapp, Information Service Branch, EPA Headquarters (202) 475-8710.

Test Methods Database

Developed by Peg Nelson of the Region 1 library, this dBASE III database indexes approved procedures for: measuring the presence and concentrations of physical and chemical pollutants; evaluating properties such as toxic properties of chemical substances or measuring the effects of substances under various conditions. A printed version of the index is available from the National Technical Information Service (NTIS) at (703) 487-4763 order number PB88-200100/AS for $14.95. For more information on a copy of the database, contact Peg Nelson at the Region 1 Library.

Hazardous Waste Collection Database

Created to provide a unified resource of major hazardous waste reports, books and journals available throughout the EPA library network, the database is the most widely-disseminated of the library network's computerized information products. Produced by the Headquarters Library, this personal computer based database contains over 3,000 pertinent citations to commercial books, EPA, Federal and Congressional reports and OSWER policy and guidance directives. State and Federal agencies can obtain copies through their Regional EPA library. The database is free to EPA staff. Printed copies are available for purchase by the general public from the National Technical Information Service at (703) 487-4763 order number PB87-152690. The price is $125 for a single copy and $325 for an annual subscription of quarterly updates. For more information contact the Headquarters Library.

EXPERTISE AND KNOWLEDGE TO SHARE

Librarians possess a storehouse of knowledge to share and do so through demonstrations, workshops and lectures.

Region 4 librarian, Gayle Alston, travels her Region informing State environmental agencies on assistance available from her library and demonstrates EPA and commercial environmental databases. Juli Sears, Region 10 librarian, also canvasses her states and provides copies of the Hazardous Waste Collection Database to waste management offices in the State agencies.

EPA librarians also help disseminate information through their own professional contacts. Peg Nelson, Region 1 librarian, Boston, has played host to the Boston Information Group (BIG), a network of corporate, State, Federal and academic information professionals. A tour of her library highlighting its special collections and databases helps to promote the information resources of all of EPA to the local community. As brokers of information, librarians also have technical expertise of their own to share:

Clearinghouses are regularly established by EPA to respond to legislative initiatives requiring the Agency to foster communications and encourage technology transfer. Most clearinghouses involve the organization of a core of substantive information and the means by which to make that information available to interested parties. The staff of the Headquarters Library recognizes the parallel concerns of libraries and clearinghouses and is available to provide advice and consultation on the development and operation of clearinghouses. To assist in the establishment of Agency sponsored clearinghouses they have prepared the following:

Bibliographic Series: Technology Transfer: Clearninghouses. EPA/IMSD/88-006. Sept. 1988

Bibliography with abstracts of recent articles on the establishment of clearinghouses, case studies, and database design and development for your clearinghouse.

Your Guide to EPA Clearinghouse and Hotlines. Oct. 1988.

A listing of key EPA sponsored clearinghouses and hotlines.

Headquarters Library: Clearinghouse Services. 1988.

Information packet containing the two clearinghouse publications listed above, plus a fact sheet describing the role and function of clearinghouses.

For more information concerning these publications contact Sheila Richard at the Headquarters Library.

Librarians also serve as a resource for their counterparts on the State and local levels. Linda Sunnen, Region 9 librarian, San Francisco, serves on the advisory group of the Information Research

Center at the University of California, Los Angeles. Funded by the National Science Foundation and part of the UCLA's School of Engineering, the Center was set up to promote engineering research for hazardous substance control. Jonda Byrd, laboratory librarian at the Andrew W. Briedenbach Environmental Research Center in Cincinnati, OH, worked with staff at the library of the Hazardous Waste Research and Information Center of the State of Illinois. The Center's mission is to assist in the reduction of environmental and health risk associated with hazardous waste through research, technical assistance and information dissemination. Working with their counterparts at these organizations, the EPA librarians suggested titles for purchase, databases to access and information dissemination techniques to practice. By working with their colleagues to educate others on the sources of technical and environmental information, EPA librarians help to increase the knowledge base for all.

For more information on the EPA Library Network, contact Brigid Rapp, Information Services Branch, IMSD, EPA Headquarters (202) 475-8710.

For a list of the EPA library closest to you and descriptions of all of the libraries in the EPA Library Network you can order the *Guide to EPA Libraries and Information Services*, EPA/IMSD/87-004, Jul. 1987, NTIS order number PB87-230173 for $13.95 by calling (703) 487-4763.

EPA NETWORK LIBRARIES

Regional Libraries

Library	Location	Telephone Number
Headquarters	Washington, DC	(202) 382-5922
Region 1	Boston, MA	(617) 565-3300
Region 2	New York, NY	(212) 264-2881
Region 3	Philadelphia, PA	(215) 597-0580
Region 4	Atlanta, GA	(404) 347-4216
Region 5	Chicago, IL	(312) 353-2022
Region 6	Dallas, TX	(214) 655-6444

Region 7	Kansas City, KS	(913) 236-2828
Region 8	Denver, CO	(303) 293-1444
Region 9	San Francisco, CA	(415) 974-8082
Region 10	Seattle, WA	(206) 442-1289

Laboratory Libraries

Library	Location	Telephone Number
Narragansett Environmental Research Laboratory	Narragansett, RI	(401) 789-1071
Region 2 Field Office	Edison, NJ	(201) 321-6762
Central Regional Laboratory	Annapolis, MD	(301) 266-9180
Library Services Office	Research Triangle Park, NC	(919) 541-2777
Sabine Island Environmental Research Laboratory	Gulf Breeze, FL	(904) 932-5311
College Station Environmental Research Laboratory	Athens, GA	(404) 546-3324
Andrew W. Briedenbach Environmental Research Center	Cincinnati, OH	(513) 569-7707
Motor Vehicle Emissions Laboratory	Ann Arbor, MI	(313) 668-4311
Duluth Environmental Research Laboratory	Duluth, MN	(218) 720-5538
Kerr Environmental Research Laboratory	Ada, OK	(405) 332-8800
Environmental Monitoring Systems Laboratory	Las Vegas, NV	(702) 798-2648
Corvallis Environmental Research Laboratory	Corvallis, OR	(503) 757-4731

Other Libraries

Law Library	Washington, DC	(202) 382-5919
Office of Non-Confidential Information Center	Washington, DC	(202) 382-3944
National Enforcement Investigation Center Library	Denver, CO	(303) 236-5122

NOTES

1. U.S. Environmental Protection Agency. *Report of the administrator's task-force on technology transfer and training*. Washington, DC: U.S. Environmental Protection Agency; 1987. 11p.

2. U.S. Environmental Protection Agency. Information Services and Library. *Technology transfer: an overview*. Washington, DC: U.S. Environmental Protection Agency; 1988. 41p.

The Center for Environmental Information: Meeting Community Information Needs

Frederick W. Stoss

SUMMARY. The Center for Environmental Information, Inc. was created in the mid-1970s as a non-profit and non-advocacy organization. Over the years the scope and nature of its programs and outreach have grown. This paper presents the history in the development of the Center and highlights the evolution of its major programs and activities.

INTRODUCTION

The Center for Environmental Information, Inc. (CEI) was established in Rochester, New York, in 1974 as an answer to the growing dilemma of where to find timely, accurate and comprehensive information on environmental issues. CEI is a private, independent, not-for-profit organization. CEI was incorporated as an educational organization, under the laws of the State of New York. It is funded by membership dues, subscription and program fees, contracts, grants and contributions. The Center receives no public funds for the general support of its library, resource center, information services or publications.

CEI's policy has always been to maintain a neutral, non-advocacy position on environmental issues, it is believed that a non-partisan and unbiased information service removes communication

---

Frederick W. Stoss is Director of Library and Information Services at the Center for Environmental Information, 99 Court Street, Rochester, NY 14608. He received the BA (Biology) at Hartwick College, the MS (Zoology) at the State University of New York College at Brockport and the MLS degree at Syracuse University. He is a past Chair of the Environmental Information Division of the Special Libraries Association.

© 1990 by The Haworth Press, Inc. All rights reserved.

barriers and can better foster an exchange of concerns and ideas among conflicting points of view. This position has allowed CEI to assist individuals, public officials, businesses and organizations to become more effective in finding constructive solutions to complex and often controversial environmental problems. This non-advocacy approach for providing services and programs has perhaps been the single most important factor assuring CEI the credibility and community support to remain a viable alternative for identifying, locating and disseminating information, and to serve the community as an unbiased forum for the discussion of environmental issues.

The Center's initial operation served Rochester and its immediate suburban areas. Soon after its founding, CEI's outreach grew to serve the region of the Western Finger Lakes and Genesee Valley. Today CEI remains a Rochester-based organization, but its services now reach far beyond the local community. This expansion of its outreach reflects the increasing number, scope and complexities of problems affecting the global environment.

FOUNDING AND EARLY HISTORY

The period of the late 1960s and early 1970s was marked by a social upheaval and awareness. The social consciousness related to ecology and the environment was sparked by the publishing of *Silent Spring*,[1] and was brought to a celebrated and festive turning point on Earth Day, April 22, 1970. On January 1 of that same year the first of a series of unprecedented legislation mandating the protection of our environment, the National Environmental Protection Act, became public law (PL 91-190, The National Environmental Protection Act of 1969). The environmental policies of this period are reflected in the first annual report of the newly formed President's Council on Environmental Quality.[2]

In February of 1973 then New York State Senator Bernard Smith and the Temporary State Commission on Youth Education in Environmental Conservation held a series of forums across the state to get public input into its program concepts. A theme expressed repeatedly was the need for improved communication and coordination among various groups and individuals involved in environmental matters. A principal recommendation made at the Rochester-based forum called for the establishment of a regional planning center or clearinghouse. This organization would serve the community-at-large to coordinate and disseminate information concerning environmental issues. The establishment of a clearinghouse was proposed to assist all segments of the community in initiating and implementing local environmental programs and activities.

While the State was investigating its expanding role in the areas of environmental and conservation education, the Monroe County Environmental Management Council (EMC)* was seeking various means of communicating more effectively to the public on the nature of its work. Elizabeth Thorndike, a member of the steering committee that planned the Rochester forum and member of the EMC's Environmental Education Committee, developed a proposal to fund an independent "environmental clearinghouse" that would coordinate communication efforts and disseminate information to the general public.

The proposal to establish the Center for Environmental Information was submitted to the EMC and the Junior League of Rochester, a womens' civic organization which provides seed money for local projects that offer volunteer leadership training and activities in community affairs.

CEI's early function was to assist the local community with a broad array of environmental questions, most of which were simple referrals to other organizations, agencies or officials. Its initial efforts were directed towards the development of a strong local environmental network of government agencies and officials, businesses and industries, organizations, academicians and concerned

---

*Section 0101-0115, Article 47 of the New York State Environmental Conservation Law, known as the Local Environmental Protection Act, authorizes the creation of county and regional environmental management councils. The councils provide environmental information to county agencies and town governments and are advisory to the county legislatures and administration. The councils are comprised of representatives from each local conservation advisory council (Section 239-X, Article 12-F of the General Municipal Law authorizes cities, towns and villages to establish these local advisory panels), members-at-large, the heads of key county agencies and county legislature members.

citizens. The establishment of this network filled a significant local void, and paved the way for CEI's future growth and expansion.

In 1978 the National Science Foundation's (NSF) Science for Citizens Program awarded CEI with a grant for the preparation of a manual that would detail the operation of the Center and assist others in developing a similar establishment. The resulting manual "Establishing an Environmental Information Center—A Guide to Organization and Operation," provided an in-depth analysis of the Center and its future.[3] The NSF grant also provided support of a study to determine how CEI could more effectively reach sectors of the community that lacked balanced information or access to information concerning policy issues that affect their daily operations or lives.

In 1980 the NSF rated CEI as one of the two top candidates for designation as a Public Service Science Center. CEI was one of 125 applicants, of which 20 were requested to submit final proposals. In 1981 funds for this project were eliminated by the Office of Management and Budget. It was noted by Elizabeth Thorndike, now the Center's Executive Director, that

> ... the designation marks the pinnacle of achievement for CEI on a national scale. There is no other recognition in our field that can top or match that accomplishment. It is an affirmation of the unique character of this organization and the community that nurtured it.[4]

GOING INTERNATIONAL WITH ACID RAIN

The national visibility created by CEI's involvement and rating by the National Science Foundation was a principal factor in attracting support from the Edison Electric Institute (EEI) and the New York State Department of Environmental Conservation (DEC) to establish the Acid Rain Information Clearinghouse (ARIC). CEI negotiated initial funding from these two groups with the necessary autonomy for the operation of ARIC.

Under provisions of the contract with the Air Resources Division of the DEC, ARIC undertook the department's role as Acid Rain Documentation Center for the Quebec-New York Agreement on

Acid Rain. In the spring of 1982, the DEC and the Quebec Ministry of Environment signed a formal Letter of Agreement, that among other provisions created a clearinghouse for identifying, gathering and disseminating information on the broad topic of acid rain. In conjunction with the Ministry ARIC expanded a core reference collection and assisted in the development of ACIDOC, a bilingual (French/English) bibliographic database devoted solely to the topic of acid rain. ACIDOC was the first bibliographic database on the topic to be offered to the public for use, and is still provided through IST-Informatheque in Montreal, Quebec.

Initial assistance with implementation of ARIC was provided by the Center for Environmental Research at Cornell University. A detailed report was prepared to design the Clearinghouse and define its operation.[5,6] The information environment for establishing such a centralized clearinghouse was ideal,[7] and allowed CEI to expand beyond its local roots.

From the onset ARIC was intentionally subject to a variety of levels of oversight. An initial 18-member Advisory Council was formed to assist ARIC in the work of the clearinghouse. This council was an international body that represented a wide variety of constituencies, disciplines and perspectives with the acidic deposition phenomenon. An additional Oversight Committee, comprised of members of CEI's Board of Directors, was formed to oversee the financing and policies of this special CEI program.

ARIC's program called for the development of a special reference library collection with particular emphasis placed on the fugitive and non-conventional information resources (state agency documents, industry reports, position papers, institutional reports, etc.). With the support of its designation as the New York Acid Rain Documentation Center this role was expanded to create the more comprehensive development of an Acid Rain Reference Collection including an extensive vertical file collection.[8]

ARIC established an on-call reference and referral service to facilitate the identification of information and resources for scientists, policy makers, attorneys, public and special interest groups, business and industry managers, environmentalists, students, sportsmen and others concerned with the topic of acid deposition. Responses to general requests are taken from the core reference collection and might consist of a statistical or documented information, a bibliographic citation for future reference or a professional contact. If the answer to the specific question is not readily at hand, a referral to a more appropriate source—agency, institution, organization, individual expert—is made.

ARIC's attempt to promote an open, interdisciplinary dialogue related to scientific and technical research and policy-making activities of governments, industries, and public interest groups is best reflected in the conferences it has sponsored. These annual events have drawn together representatives from the full spectrum of viewpoints and have stimulated a cross-disciplinary exchange of information and ideas on the topic of acid rain. The following list of conference titles suggests the focus of ARIC's programming:

- Acid Rain: A New York Agenda
- Acid Rain: An Economic Perspective
- Liming Acidic Waters: Environmental and Policy Concerns
- Acid Rain: The Relationship Between Sources and Receptors
- Acid Rain: The View from the States
- Global Climate Change Linkages: Acid Rain, Air Quality and Stratospheric Ozone Depletion
- Acid Rain Research in New York

To fulfil its commitment to disseminate information on the topic of acid rain to a broad, multi-disciplinary audience, ARIC began the publication of the *Acid Precipitation Digest*. This monthly current awareness bulletin provides a concise compilation of current news, bibliographic citations and events related to the topic of acidic deposition. Beginning with the sixth volume (1988) the *Digest* is published by Elsevier Science Publishing Company (New York). In its first six issues (1983-1988) the *Digest* has described more than 8,000 individual information items.

With the transfer of the publication of the *Acid Precipitation Digest* came the addition of another title to be produced by CEI for publication by Elsevier—the *Global Climate Change Digest*. Modeled after the *Acid Precipitation Digest*, this second current awareness bulletin is a monthly consolidated source for research and policy information on the causes, effects and responses to global climate changes that are caused by human industrial activity and man-made chemical compounds. Each issue describes information on the topics of stratospheric ozone depletion (the so-called "ozone hole" phenomenon) and global warming through the continuing build-up of atmospheric carbon dioxide, chlorofluorocarbons, methane and other "greenhouse" gases.

In response producing this new publication and expanding its scope of coverage, the Acid Rain Information Clearinghouse changed its name to the Air Resource Information Clearinghouse in 1989. Major collection development into these additional areas of concern will take place when the required funding is achieved.

CEI ORGANIZATION

The day-to-day operation of CEI is supervised by a full-time Executive Vice President. The President, CEI's founder and former Executive Director, is responsible for the overall administration and oversight of the organization, and is responsible to the Board of Directors. All program directors (Fund Development, Operations, and Library and Information Services) report to the Executive Vice President with all editorial staff reporting to the President.

The formal duty of the Board of Directors is to set CEI policy. It has other functions that assure the financial well-being and professional integrity of the organization and staff and the assures CEI's professional interactions with other groups. Second only to CEI's non-advocacy position in sustaining broad, long-term community support for CEI, has been the dedication of the Board of Directors in fulfilling their duties. The diverse and balanced representation of its board has allayed suspicions among various constituents of the community, and allowed CEI to grow to its present size and stature. An Advisory Council is appointed by the Board of Directors to provide technical and professional consultation to CEI and its staff.

To meet the growing needs for current and comprehensive information, CEI has developed a multi-faceted program. CEI's activities are geared to meet the specific needs of researchers and policy makers as well as the general needs of the student or concerned citizen.

CEI disseminates information through a number of publications, including an environmental newspaper, *Upstate Environment*. This bi-monthly publication is distributed mostly in the Rochester—Finger Lakes—Genesee region of western New York. It carries major local, state, national and international news and features. It provides comprehensive coverage of local issues and perspectives of state, national and global issues.

A bi-monthly newsletter, the *CEI Sphere*, describes for its members a behind-the-scenes look at the extended activities of CEI, its staff, board members and volunteers.

CEI's annual *Directory of Environmental Agencies and Organizations* is a guide to more than 400 groups, agencies and organizations in a 12-county region of New York. For more than 13 years this directory has served as the core for a rather well established environmental network in the region.

More recently CEI has produced various reports under contract to private organizations and public agencies. A *Self- Study Guide for Commercial Pesticide Applicators* was prepared under a contract with the New York State Department of Environmental Conservation. Under a contract with one of New York's electrical utilities, CEI produces a quarterly report series that summarizes the most current information related to the environmental and policy concerns associated with the incineration of municipal solid wastes. A grant with the Region II Office of the Environmental Protection Agency saw the production of a technical report, *Identification of Potential Small Quantity Generators of Hazardous Waste and Implementing a Pilot Training Workshop in Monroe and Livingston Counties of Upstate New York*. CEI has also produced independently a special report, *Energy Use in Monroe County—An Assessment of the Present and Proposals for the Future*.

One of the principal means for stimulating discussion and debate on environmental issues has been through the sponsorship of conferences, seminars and other education programs. These events are geared for an audience representing a wide range of viewpoints and perspectives. In addition to its annual air resources-related programs, major conferences sponsored by CEI in the past several years include the following:

- The Impact of Environmental Regulations on Real Estate Transactions (Rochester, NY)
- Land Preservation Techniques: Review of Mechanisms (Rochester, NY)

- Training Workshop for Small Quantity Generators of Hazardous Waste (Rochester, NY)
- Biotechnology: Science and Policy (Albany, NY)
- Environment 2000: Setting Our Sights for a Sustainable Future (Rochester, NY)
- Environment 2000: Governor's Conference on the Environment (New York, NY)
- Environmental Regulation and the Small Business (Rochester, NY)
- Biotechnology: Challenges and Promises (Rochester, NY)

One of the more popular programs offered by CEI is its Annual Survey Course in Environmental Law. This course is designed to provide a general overview of environmental law and recent developments on the local, state and federal levels. The program concentrates on the history and philosophy behind current environmental law, major problem areas and unresolved issues, and possible future directions of the law. The course is co-sponsored by the Monroe County Bar Association, and has been developed to meet the needs of local government officials, attorneys, engineers, business and industry managers, and the interested public.

Throughout the year CEI convenes quarterly, informal, noontime seminars, Timely Topics, on subjects of immediate interest or importance. In recent years this lecture series has included the following topics:

- Asbestos in the Home
- Doing the Lake Ontario RAP (Remedial Action Plan)
- Protecting New York's Heritage—The Environmental Quality Bond Act
- Radon—Cause for Concern?
- Halving Our Trash—The DEC's Solid Waste Management Plan
- China—Environmental Challenges vs. Economic Imperatives
- Protecting Coastal Habitats
- Toxic Chemical and the Environment
- Congress and the Environment

At the heart of CEI's operation is its reference library collection. This non-circulating collection is open to the public and consists of more than 10,000 volumes. The collection is comprised of typical monographs—research reports, proceedings, and books with a special emphasis on nonconventional materials produced by local and state governments, foundations, research centers, special and public interest groups. The shelved collection is supplemented by more than 24 vertical file drawers of reprints, clippings, pamphlets, flyers and brochures covering more than 400 topics of local to global interest.

The library subscribes to 200 serials. A core collection of technical and professional journals is supplemented by a variety of environmental newspapers, magazines, trade publications, newsletters, serial reports and other publications. This serials collection does not overlap significantly with the technical journals found in the public and academic libraries in the region. When necessary, referral to these more technical collections is made. It is interesting, however, to note that a large number of CEI's library visitors are students and faculty of local colleges and universities seeking to supplement information gathered at their own academic libraries.

In addition to hundreds of local visits per year to the library by area residents or visitors to the Rochester area, CEI responds to thousands of requests for information from around the world. Its own library resources are supplemented through its access to a variety of other libraries in the immediate Rochester area. CEI's access to regional resources was enhanced greatly through its membership in the Rochester Regional Library Council.

CEI's library and resource center is staffed by one professional librarian, two para-professional information specialists and several extremely loyal and dedicated volunteers that have included chemists, engineers, researchers and librarians. Whenever possible CEI encourages student interns working in the library. These interns include graduate and undergraduate students from local colleges and universities that are seeking future employment in an environmental setting, and graduate library students from Syracuse University and the State University of New York at Buffalo.

The library maintains an on-call reference and referral service during normal business hours. Simple reference requests are handled through written or phone inquiries and walk-in visits. General ready-reference questions are provided free of charge. More complex information requests are performed as a fee-based, cost-recovery service. One of the areas of potential growth for CEI's information services is to the small business community, especially the testing, consulting and legal segments.

WHAT LIES AHEAD

CEI was founded in 1974 in the midst of confusion and controversy concerning information requirements for all segments of the community concerned with environmental issues. The organization was developed to promote community understanding of our natural environment and to provide comprehensive information to those charged with making decisions about the environment. It has served as a forum for the interdisciplinary exchange of information among experts representing diverse points of view.

For 15 years CEI has tried to encourage coordinated efforts among governments, industries and the public. Its scope of activity has expanded from a local focus to more global dissemination of information. That CEI has been sustained for 15 years is testimony of its success and effectiveness.

The Center for Environmental Information is filling a niche in the full spectrum of institutions which seek the protection of the environment. CEI is ever hopeful that as we begin the last decade of the 20th Century, it will be fortunate to continue to serve as a viable alternative source of information concerning the environment, not only for Rochester, but for the "global community," as well.

REFERENCES

1. Carson, Rachel. *Silent spring*. Boston: Houghton Mifflin Company; 1962. 368p.
2. Council on Environmental Quality. *Environmental quality: the first annual report of the Council on environmental quality*. Washington, DC: US Government Printing Office; 1970. 326p.
3. Thorndike, Elizabeth. *Establishing an environmental information center*. Prepared on National Science Foundation Grant #OSS78-21721. Rochester, NY: Center for Environmental Information, Inc.; 1978. 95p.
4. Hartwell, Reginald W. *CEI decade: glimpses of a phenomenon in the making – a history of the Center for Environmental Information, Inc., 1974-1984*. Rochester, NY: Center for Environmental Information, Inc.; 1984. 56p.
5. Dosa, Marta; Stoss, Frederick W. *Development of an acid rain information*

clearinghouse. Syracuse, NY: School of Information Studies, Syracuse University; 1982. 87p.

6. Dosa, Marta; Stoss, Frederick W. Information management at an acid rain information clearinghouse. In: American Society for Information Science. *Proceedings of the 46th ASIS Annual Meeting on Productivity in the Information Age, held in Washington, DC on October 2-6. 1983*. Washington, DC: ASIS; 1983; p. 248-251.

7. Trumbule, Robert E.; Tedeschi, Marilyn. Acid rain information: knee deep and rising. *Science & Technology Libraries*. 4(2):27-41; 1984.

8. Lovenburg, Susan L.; Stoss, Frederick W. The fugitive literature of acid rain: making use of nonconventional information sources in a vertical file. *RSR (Reference Services Review)*. 16(1-2):95-104; 1988.

Environmental Publications of the American Chemical Society

Maureen Welling Matkovich

SUMMARY. The American Chemical Society integrates the publishing of environmental information into its regular publications programs. Its publications programs produce scholarly books and journals, newsletters, meeting abstracts and preprints of extended abstracts, as well as information pamphlets and booklets for general distribution.

INTRODUCTION

The American Chemical Society publishes or distributes considerable amounts of information about chemicals in the environment. Much of this material is offered for sale in the annual publications catalog and can be identified by consulting standard bibliographic sources. Other publications, if not precisely vertical file material, belong to the class of gray literature or fugitive material which so very often defies the identification and acquisition efforts of librarians. In contrast to corporate gray literature, the American Chemical Society's publications in this category are usually intended for the widest possible distribution. Single copies of these publications are often free; multiple copies or subscriptions have only nominal charges and, in many cases, there is explicit permission to photoduplicate if proper credit is given. A third publication type, which falls somewhere between formally published and readily identifiable materials listed for sale in the publications catalog and the fugi-

---

Maureen W. Matkovich is Manager, Library Services, American Chemical Society, 1155 Sixteenth Street NW, Washington, DC 20036. She received the BS (Chemistry) degree at Ohio University and the MLS and PhD (Inorganic chemistry) degrees at the University of Kentucky.

© 1990 by The Haworth Press, Inc. All rights reserved.

tive literature consist of publications of the thirty-two membership divisions. The formality of the divisional publication programs varies from division to division. This paper will document these various types of publications, but with a disproportionate emphasis on the divisional and fugitive literature because, from the author's experience, these areas cause the most confusion. The paper will not address the secondary sources published by Chemical Abstracts Service, the abstracting and indexing service, which is a division of the American Chemical Society.

FORMAL PUBLICATIONS

Although other American Chemical Society (ACS) primary journals do cover environmental chemistry, *Environmental Science and Technology* (ES&T) is the core ACS journal in this area. It is a monthly publication which started in 1967. In addition to research papers, ES&T publishes feature articles, opinion columns, occasional book reviews, meeting announcements, and business and regulatory news. ES&T is indexed in its entirety by *Applied Science and Technology Index*; it is selectively indexed by the *Abstract Bulletin of the Institute of Paper Chemistry, Bibliography of Agriculture, Biological Abstracts,* and *Chemical Abstracts*.

Chemical and Engineering News, the weekly news magazine of the ACS, also carries environmental (particularly regulatory) news in its business and government concentrates. Its ACS meeting briefs (programs) announce and document papers presented at the Society's regional and national meetings. Programs of additional conferences and symposia that are sponsored or cosponsored by ACS divisions are announced here. ACS news stories will often announce publication of additions to the fugitive literature such as the booklets discussed later in this article. *Chemical and Engineering News* is indexed in its entirety by *Applied Science and Technology Index, Business Periodicals Index,* and *Trade and Industry Index*. It is indexed selectively by *Chemical Industry Notes, CIS Abstracts, Biological Abstracts* and *Engineering Index. Chemical and Engineering News* also has its own index (sold separately) which covers the magazine in great detail.

The American Chemical Society is an important publisher of

books and monographs on the chemical sciences. The Advances in Chemistry Series, the ACS Symposium Series, and the ACS Monograph Series are numbered series which are published by the books department. Professional reference books and books that are semitechnical or nontechnical discussions of scientific topics are also part of the formal book publishing program.

According to Robin Giroux, ACS acquisitions editor, the Advances in Chemistry Series

> is composed of monographic volumes that are multiauthored with an overall editor or editors. Advances in Chemistry Series volumes are classic in nature and lasting in value; they address fairly mature topics and serve as reference works for several years. Chapters in these books are of high scientific quality and contain substantial review material. After complete peer review, these chapters are edited and typeset. Titles in this series may derive from symposia.

For an example, the first volume of this series, published in 1949, was *Agricultural Control Chemicals*. It contains the collected papers from the Symposia on Economic Poisons presented before the Division of Agricultural and Food Chemistry at the 115th and 116th national ACS meetings. The newest title is number 220, *Archaeological Chemistry IV*, 1988. Despite the first volume in the series, there are only a few titles which cover chemicals in the environment. Of these, the largest number treat pollutants in water.

To quote Robin Giroux again,

> the ACS Symposium Series provides a format for rapid publication of books that cover topics of current interest, in fields in which information is expanding quickly. Most of these books are developed from symposia. However, they are not simply proceedings because additional material is often added to the books to enhance the comprehensiveness of the subject coverage. Such additions may include review material, tutorial chapters, additional chapters, or even glossaries. After the chapters have undergone limited peer review, they are prepared in camera-ready format by the authors.

Volume 1, published in 1974, was entitled *Approaches to Automotive Emissions Control*. It was the proceedings of a symposium cosponsored by the Division of Fuel Chemistry and the Division of Petroleum Chemistry at the 167th Meeting of the ACS. The newest title, *Biogenic Sulfur in the Environment*, number 393, is the proceedings of a symposium sponsored by the Division of Environmental Chemistry in 1987. One can categorize the subjects of the approximately forty environmental titles as covering pesticides and agricultural chemicals, the chemistry of fuels with the problems of acid rain and air pollution, and techniques for the analysis of environmental chemicals. All of these books were written primarily for the experts although some of them may contain enough supplementary material to be of limited interest to others.

Because ACS divisions negotiate publication rights independently, a significant number of their sponsored symposia are published by publishers other than the American Chemical Society. The secretaries of the various divisions usually maintain lists of the publishers of their divisions' symposia.

The third numbered series is the ACS Monograph Series. The series was initiated in 1919 at the Interallied Conference of Pure and Applied Chemistry. The original publisher was the Chemical Catalog Company and the first title was *Chemistry of Enzyme Actions*. The first edition has an imprint of 1921. The series was published by Reinhold for many years. The ACS started publishing this series with number 170. According to the 1989 publications catalog, this series is intended "to make available to chemists a thorough treatment of a selected area in a form usable by persons working in more or less unrelated fields to the end that they may correlate their own work with a large area of physical science discipline" and "to stimulate further research in the specific field treated." They are scholarly summaries of the subject. This series contains no volumes with a clear environmental orientation although the second edition of *Chemical Carcinogens* (no. 182: 1984) does treat some naturally occurring carcinogens in the environment.

ACS Professional Reference Books is a new unnumbered imprint. Handbooks, dictionaries and other books intended for desk use by practicing chemists are published as professional reference books. Environmental titles include *Principles of Environmental*

Sampling and *Kinetics of Environmental Aquatic Photochemistry: Theory and Practice*.

Next, the ACS publishes some general interest science books. *Silent Spring Revisited* (1987) is an example of an environmental title which is intended for nonchemists who are interested in scientific issues discussed at a semitechnical level as well as chemists who are not expert in the specific subject. This particular title is the proceedings of a symposium sponsored by the Pesticide Subcommittee of the ACS Committee on Environmental Improvement in 1984. It summarizes technical and political aspects of the pesticide debate beginning with the publication of Rachel Carlson's *Silent Spring* in 1962.[1]

ENVIRONMENTAL INFORMATION FOR WIDER DISTRIBUTION

Numerous American Chemical Society publications are intended for wide distribution at nominal cost to the user. They may or may not be copyrighted. Their publication has been supported by grants or by the Society as a whole. They generally do not have ISBNs or ISSNs and are not included in the publications catalog. Many of them are on environmental or regulatory topics. They are neither in-depth studies of the issues nor manuals for regulatory compliance. However, these booklets concisely introduce the subjects and usually provide excellent lists of sources of additional information including standard literature references, emergency phone numbers (hotlines), addresses of government offices, and information about other hard-to-find documents published by foundations, associations and government agencies. The descriptions of these booklets in the list below are quoted from their introductions or prefaces.

Chemical Risk Communication: Preparing for Community Interest in Chemical Release Data; Department of Government Relations and Science Policy: 1988. A twenty-eight-page booklet prepared by ACS volunteers, led by William Beranek, Jr. and funded by the Alfred P. Sloan Foundation. Its purpose is

> to present a basic understanding of risk assessment concepts and risk communication techniques that can be used as a

framework when responding to questions from the public about releases of chemicals to the environment . . . [for] persons who bear the publication communication obligations, those to whom citizens and the news media will turn with questions and concerns: local public health officials and other local leaders.

Copyright notice. Single copies free.

Issues in Peer Review of the Scientific Basis for Regulatory Decisions; Department of Government Relations and Science Policy and The Conservation Foundation: 1985. A thirty-one-page booklet sponsored by the Council on Environmental Quality and financed by the Environmental Protection Agency. It was written by William Beranek, Jr. (ACS Committee on Environmental Improvement), J. Clarence Davies (The Conservation Foundation), and Susan Moses (ACS staff). It defines peer review and discusses options and guidelines for formulating regulations. Single copies free.

Less Is Better: Laboratory Chemical Management for Waste Reduction; Department of Government Relations and Science Policy: 1985. A sixteen-page booklet prepared by the Subcommittee on Alternative Waste Management to the ACS Task Force on RCRA.

Intended for those persons responsible for managing laboratory hazardous waste chemicals . . . chemists at the bench, professors and science teachers, research directors and laboratory managers . . . five sections that address waste reduction through management techniques such as purchasing control, inventory control, surplus chemical exchange, reclamation, and recycling.

Copyright notice. Single copies free.

RCRA and Laboratories; Department of Government Relations and Science Policy: 1986. Revised by the ACS Task Force on RCRA. A twenty-four-page booklet "intended to aid generators of laboratory wastes in determining their responsibilities for proper disposal of hazardous wastes under the developing RCRA regulations." Copyright notice. Single copies free.

The Department of Government Relations and Science Policy started to publish a series of information pamphlets in 1982. Most of these unnumbered pamphlets are on environmental issues. In these pamphlets, the ACS attempts to increase the understanding of the chemistry (its capabilities as well as its limitations) behind the science-related controversies and regulatory issues. These pamphlets are generally written under the auspices of the ACS Committee on Environmental Improvement. In certain aspects, these pamphlets continue and update two major reports issued by the Committee on Environmental Improvement in the 1970s. These reports were *Cleaning Our Environment: The Chemical Basis for Action* (1971) and the second edition, *Cleaning Our Environment: A Chemical Perspective* (1978). The publications have copyright notices, but also specifically allow photoduplication. Single copies free.

Acid Rain: 1982; rev. 1985. An eight-page pamphlet originally written by Robert A. Fitzgerald which "focuses on the need for a better understanding of the chemistry of pollutants released into the atmosphere and the resulting acidic fallout."

Chemical Risk: A Primer: 1984. A twelve-page pamphlet written by Susan Moses which "focuses primarily on the scientific issues involved in determining the health risks arising from exposure to chemicals . . . an introduction to the controversial science/art of determining risk."

Ground Water: 1983. A fourteen-page pamphlet written by Terri A. Nally which "presents fundamental concepts concerning the chemistry of ground water and begins to build a basis from which citizens can evaluate information about ground-water problems, construct plans of action, and gauge the implications of that action."

Hazardous Waste Management: 1984. A twelve-page pamphlet written by Terri A. Nally and Jean A. Parr which describes "within a chemical context, the nature of the issue [hazardous waste management] . . . the sources of complexities and uncertainties, and some potential solutions that are currently practiced in managing the hazardous wastes that are being generated."

Pesticides: 1987. A twelve-page pamphlet written by Jean A. Parr which discusses "the basic facts about pesticide usage and outlines management practices that may be employed to achieve a more effective use of these chemical tools while minimizing exposure to their potentially harmful side-effects."

Two additional pamphlets will be available in 1989: *Chemical Risks: Personal Decisions* and *Global Climate Change*.

The Department of Government Relations and Science Policy also conducts workshops at regional meetings. A collection of presentations made at forums on "Hazardous Waste Management at Academic Institutions" is available. Finally, the Department of Government Relations and Science Policy has published *Network News* since 1987. It is a newsletter designed for academic institutions which often covers hazardous waste disposal regulations as they apply to colleges and universities.

DIVISIONAL PUBLICATIONS

American Chemical Society divisions are generally organized around the various subdisciplines of chemistry. These divisions may carry out publications programs which are completely independent of the Society's overall publication efforts. Generally, these publications fall into two categories: (1) Preprints of papers presented at numbered national meetings and other symposia and conferences sponsored by the divisions and (2) Divisional newsletters.

The Division of Water and Waste Chemistry was founded in 1913, but first started formally collecting and printing preprints of the technical papers presented at the national meetings in 1961. This Division changed its name to the Division of Environmental Chemistry in 1975. The current preprints of the extended abstracts are abstracted by *Chemical Abstracts* and are available from the secretary of the Division. Like all meeting preprints, it may be impossible to acquire copies of these extended abstracts after the meeting. Advance notice of the programs for the national meetings is given regularly in *Chemical and Engineering News* and may be of some help in identifying and acquiring these preprints. The Division also semiannually publishes a newsletter, *EnviroFACTS*, which carries the standard divisional business and awards reports, calls for papers, and programs of upcoming meetings.

There are two additional print sources of papers presented at the meetings which will be briefly mentioned. Compilations of abstracts of the papers to be presented at numbered national meetings are sold by the American Chemical Society. For the Division of Environmental Chemistry, these abstracts are not usually important because of the existence of the preprints of the extended abstracts.

To digress briefly, there have been two numbered national ACS meetings per year since the first national meeting in 1890 except that there were no numbered meetings held in 1945 and there were three numbered meetings held in 1964. There was an extra unnumbered meeting held in 1966. Congresses sponsored in cooperation with other scientific organizations may or may not be ACS numbered meetings although many of its divisions may organize technical programs. For example, the Third Chemical Congress of North America, held in Toronto in June, 1988, was also the 195th meeting of the ACS. However, the International Chemical Congress of Pacific Basin Societies, scheduled for December 1989 in Honolulu is not a numbered meeting. For a discussion of the organization as well as the history of the ACS, see *A Century of Chemistry: The Role of Chemists and the American Chemical Society*.[2]

The ACS also sponsors a maximum of ten regional meetings a year in which environmental chemistry papers may be presented. Books of these abstracts are available at the meeting itself and often, but not always, can be acquired from the program chairman. Again, *Chemical and Engineering News* carries the advance programs and names of the organizers of these regional meetings.

CONCLUSION

In conclusion, the American Chemical Society has many diverse publication efforts. Environmental information ranges from scholarly reports of new research through publications designed to increase public understanding of environmental chemistry to news coverage of regulatory actions. The formats include scholarly journals, newsletters and magazines, books, pamphlets, and presentations of papers at national and regional meetings.

REFERENCES

1. Carson, Rachel. *Silent Spring*. New York: Houghton; 1962. 368p.
2. Reese, K. M., ed. *A century of chemistry: the role of chemists and the American Chemical Society*. Washington: American Chemical Society; 1976. 468p.

Adirondack Research Center: Research Resource on the Adirondacks

Maryde F. King

SUMMARY. The Adirondack Research Center was established to protect, centralize and make available to researchers the voluminous documentary history on the Adirondacks. Most notable is the collection on history of the conservation movement in the Adirondacks including the politics and government conservation and legislation and its effect on the people and the social histories of the region. Much of the conservation effort as recorded in these documents was focused on saving or protecting the environment through the official care and protection of the Adirondack natural resources. Conservation concerns have evolved into the encompassing interest and concern for the total environment of the Adirondacks as reflected in current documents and legislation.

I. ADIRONDACK RESEARCH CENTER BACKGROUND

In 1870, a land surveyor from Albany, New York, named Verplanck Colvin, stood on the summit of Mt. Seward in the Adirondacks and was bothered by the "chopping and burning off of vast tracts of forest in the wilderness" and wrote that the "remedy for this is the creation of an Adirondack park or timber preserve..." Conservation in the Adirondacks is primarily concerned with the most efficient use of the natural resources, watershed and timber, and the protection of these resources from abuse and waste. The Adirondacks perform the function of a storehouse for fresh water for the reservoirs and waterways such as the Hudson River and the

---

Maryde F. King received a BA (Chemistry) from Whitman College and the MLS degree from the University of Washington. She was manager of the Whitney Library at the General Electric Research and Development Center until her retirement in 1987.

© 1990 by The Haworth Press, Inc. All rights reserved.

Erie Canal. Environmental trends in the Adirondacks in the late nineteenth century, such as the fires that often followed logging operations and spraying sparks from the early steam engines on the railroads through the mountains, denuded vast acreages in the Adirondacks causing catastrophic changes in the Adirondack environment.

Laborious research by Adirondack historians, scientists and writers provide good background on the environment of the Adirondacks and its effect on the lives of the people through the years. Volumes such as *A History of the Adirondacks*, by Alfred L. Donaldson and *Fifty Years of Conservation in New York State*, by Gurth Whipple represent the gleanings of many years. The second volume of Donaldson's *History* includes an excellent comprehensive bibliography. This bibliography was brought up-to-date in 1958 through the efforts of a large committee under the direction of librarians Dorothy A. Plum of Vassar College Library and Lynette L. Scribner from the New York Public Library. It was entitled *Adirondack Bibliography* and published by the Adirondack Mountain Club, Inc. A supplement was later published, bringing the bibliography coverage up to 1965.

The conservation of natural resources as a means of maintaining good environmental ambience is of primary interest to the residents of New York State. Citizen efforts to maintain or improve their environment have both local and national and sometimes international significance. Acid rain effects can be traced from varied and distant sources. Statistics and background information for comparisons and education on environmental degradation are recorded in official New York State documents as well as the guidebooks written over the years for the hikers and tourists and the hunters and fishermen who regularly visited the area.

II. ADIRONDACK RESEARCH CENTER COLLECTION

The Adirondack Research Center collection's special strength is in the voluminous records of the various commissions, associations and agencies whose primary responsibility has been Adirondack issues. The history of the conservation movement in the Adirondacks, including politics and government conservation and legislation and the records of the general social histories of the Adirondack region form the basis of the collection. Such records provide the environmentalist with bench mark data for studies on air and water quality and the effects of pollution on the exhaustion of natural resources such as the diminishing quality of the forests; the reduction of bird and animal life; and the reduced sightings or disappearance of protected native plant species. The impact of increased population and development on natural resources and the wildlife habitat can be studied and comparisons made using these resources.

The collection also includes archive materials from the personal files of Adirondack conservationists John Apperson and Louis Marshall and the records of the Association for the Protection of the Adirondacks. Unpublished records of interest and value are a unique part of the Adirondack Research Center's collection efforts, such as the complete legal file of the Panther Mountain Dam battle. The Archives of the Association for the Protection of the Adirondacks includes reports, letters, maps, conference proceedings and other records pertaining to every substantial issue which has confronted the Adirondack Park and the Forest Preserve since 1901 when the Association was founded. These archives have been organized and indexed providing access to these valuable files.

Environmentalist John S. Apperson's efforts to save the high peaks of the Adirondacks from lumbering and the resulting destructive erosion are a part of the Adirondack Research Center's collection. The papers and photographs documenting this work have been arranged chronologically and an index is being compiled. Louis Marshall worked for conservation issues at the New York State and the federal level during the period of 1916 to 1930. Important records covering Louis Marshall's significant work on conservation are indexed and are part of the resources available for studying environmental and conservation issues.

The American Wildlife Research Foundation supports the collection by providing useful research materials on wildlife in the Adirondack and Catskill mountains. Publications such as the Department of Environmental Conservation's Unit Management Plans, seminal works on the life history of species such as the White-tailed deer and Ruffed grouse and the studies of Dr. William

Porter, Co-director of the Adirondack Ecological Center of the State University of New York's School of Environmental Science and Forestry are funded by the American Wildlife Research Foundation. The resource materials used by Louis C. Curth in writing his history of the New York State's ranger force, entitled *The Forest Rangers* (1987), is a new valued addition to the Adirondack Research Center's archives.

III. RESEARCH USE OF THE COLLECTION

The *Adirondack Bibliography* provides quick and often detailed access to the publications, articles, documents and maps relating to Adirondack concerns. Since 1872, New York State has been concerned with conservation or the planned management of natural resources of the Adirondacks in relation to the environment or the surroundings of the area. The *Adirondack Bibliography* is organized for browsing in broad subject areas such as history, geography, conservation, natural history, social and economic history, health and medicine, religious history, education, recreation and associated organizations, biography and Adirondack art and literature. This book also is supplied with an excellent specific index leading the researcher to specific authors and people as well as locating publications on named reservoirs, rivers or mountains. The Adirondack Research Center is cooperating with others interested in bringing the book up-to-date since many of the resource publications on the Adirondacks are not included in the current on-line indexing services. The Governor of New York State has recently appointed a Commission on the Adirondacks for the Twenty-first Century. This committee will be working in Albany, New York, and is planning to use the Adirondack Research Center's collection for background information on the Adirondacks in order to study trends and make comparisons with the environment of earlier times with the environment of today and to work on the planned management of the natural resources for the overall benefit of the people of the state.

Early maps are a rich resource of detailed information on the population density, the location of mills and businesses as well as the roads, bridges, dams and streams, ponds and canals. Some of the early maps also provide the family names for each residence as well. Villages appeared and disappeared as the industry in an area changed. Much of this type of information can be obtained from careful study of early maps. Some communities were fortunate enough to have a local historian who recorded in detail the activities of the community. For many years mining was one of the primary industries in the Adirondacks. Today there is a limited amount of mining activity. The timber industry is still a primary business in the Adirondacks, although year-round tourism and recreation are becoming one of the primary employers in the Adirondacks. The New York State and government documents describe and record the changes in these business activities over the years so that previous trends can be studied and projections for the future of the Adirondacks can be made. The effects of population growth on an area and the pressure of increased traffic can be studied to determine the environmental impact. Acid rain has already had an impact on the lakes and streams of the Adirondacks because the bedrock and soil of the area is primarily anorthosite, which is composed of feldspar (basically aluminum silicate). Acid rains are somewhat neutralized where the primary bedrock is composed of limestone, consisting mainly of calcium carbonate.

IV. COOPERATION WITH OTHER RESEARCH AND EDUCATIONAL GROUPS

The dissemination of environmental information and education is a large assignment. The Adirondack Research Center cooperates with many area organizations in the presentation of programs and sharing of information resources. The Environmental Clearinghouse of Schenectady was founded in 1972 and is a non-profit organization whose purpose is to provide information concerning the environment and to offer opportunities for experiencing the natural area of the region. The projects of the Environmental Clearinghouse of Schenectady are planned and executed by a volunteer Board of Directors, assisted by staff members and the active participation of its 500 members. The activities are supported by the members through membership fees and special contribution. Education on environmental issues is served by a 24-hour answering service for environmental questions as well as special slide programs and presentations.

The Adirondack Council was founded in 1975 and is dedicated to preserving and enhancing the Adirondack Park through public education, advocacy, and legal action when necessary. The Adirondack Council is funded entirely by membership and private foundations. The Adirondack Council is currently sponsoring a series of publications entitled *2020 VISION*. This is a series of reports setting forth a vision for the Adirondack Park of the year 2020 and beyond. Subjects to be covered include biological diversity, wilderness and wild forest (the two main categories of the Adirondack Forest Preserve), lakes and lake shores, recreational road and river corridors, economics and park management. These studies are designed to provide a specific and comprehensive plan for the Adirondack Park. *2020 VISION* has the subtitle, *Fulfilling the Promise of the Adirondack Park*. This goal is to present a plan to New York State to guarantee the preservation and ecological integrity of this superb natural resource.

As well as working with the Adirondack Council, the Adirondack Research Center also works with the Adirondack Mountain Club, Inc. The creed of the Adirondack Mountain Club is as follows:

> I believe in the Out-of-Doors, the woods, streams, and hills, the wild life that lives therein; I believe that man's care for them in a state of nature consistent with conservation is his best investment for the future.

Educational and conservation programs are one of the primary activities of the Adirondack Mountain Club. Two 16 mm color films *Lake George Country* and *Of Rivers and Men* were made available for loan from the Schenectady Chapter of the Adirondack Mountain Club as part of their effort to increase public awareness of the values of our natural heritage. Symposia, seminars and lectures are often co-sponsored with these groups to promote environmental education. Many of these organizations maintain libraries and files of resource materials on the environment which are shared or disseminated for increased availability to the public.

The Adirondack Research Center is a young organization endeavoring to provide a means of studying and assessing the environmental protection of the Adirondacks through the collection and organization of the many publications on Adirondack issues from the earliest times to the present and making this resource available to all researchers.

Current Awareness Objective of Reference Serial Focusing on Environmental Issues: A Look at *Environmental Periodicals Bibliography*

Joanne St. John

SUMMARY. This secondary information service, initiated in the early 1970s, arose out of a need for rapid dissemination of new information on environmental issues. Its scope is international, and its style of organization lends itself to use by undergraduates, practitioners, and concerned laypersons as well as sophisticated searchers. An easy-to-use natural language index, plus listings of full tables of contents of more than 350 scientific, technical, and socially-oriented journals, combine to make this a particularly accessible reference tool. The role of such secondary reference serials in the sciences is increasingly significant in light of escalating periodicals prices and frozen or reduced library budgets.

OUTGROWTH OF ENVIRONMENTAL CRISIS

In January 1969 the beautiful Santa Barbara Channel off California's central coast was the site of the world's first major oil spill. The awful consequences of this event were indelibly impressed on millions of television viewers who witnessed the damage. A new environmental consciousness emerged, reflecting awareness that the man-made disaster off the California coast would probably not be unique. The accuracy of that unhappy prediction was made

---

Joanne St. John earned baccalaureate degrees in English and Anthropology from the University of California at Los Angeles. She is a consultant in publications and marketing, and serves the International Academy at Santa Barbara as Vice President and Publisher of its several reference serials.

© 1990 by The Haworth Press, Inc. All rights reserved.

abundantly clear in 1989 when an Exxon supertanker spilled one-fifth of its cargo, more than 10 million gallons of crude, into Alaska's Prince William Sound, causing devastation on an unprecedented scale.

One inevitable result of the 1969 oil spill was a burgeoning literature focusing on such issues as petroleum exploration and exploitation of natural resources. Articles on fossil fuels and other "environmental" topics appeared in scientific, technical, and popular print media, and a specialized genre flourished: environmental periodicals.

Santa Barbara, California, became a mecca for environmentalists and for movements related to their causes. One local resident, appalled by the terrible damage of the '69 spill and by the prospect of future disasters, decided to address the problem by creating a medium for rapid dissemination of bibliographic information about currently published articles on environmental topics. As the founder and then president of a Santa Barbara-based scholarly publishing company, ABC-CLIO, Eric Boehm had a strong background in the creation of secondary reference services. His publishing company had grown up around an abstracting service he had created for historians and other humanists, *Historical Abstracts*.

Boehm brought to the environmental publishing project a deep personal interest, his background in reference publishing, and a small, decade-old nonprofit educational institution which he had founded. Devoted to dissemination of information on current affairs, the International Academy at Santa Barbara had sponsored a series of lectures on topics of local, national, and international concern. The environment was a logical focus for the Academy, and publishing a natural extension of its earlier information dissemination efforts.

With these credentials, plus an appreciation of the important and growing role that computers could play in indexing, Boehm was well positioned to tackle the field of environmental information. The tiny and impecunious Academy had only the most limited resources to pour into the ambitious new publishing venture. The first volume of what was to become *Environmental Periodicals Bibliography* was modestly produced in 1972 under the title *Environmental*

Periodicals. It consisted of eight issues of photo-reproduced tables of contents from environmentally-focused periodicals.

FOCUS ON ACCESSIBILITY OF INFORMATION

With the first volume under their belts, Boehm and the small staff working on what was now called *Environmental Periodicals Bibliography (EPB)* introduced some refinements in the fledgling bibliographic publication. Their continuing goals were to be as current as possible, minimizing lag time between the original publication of an article and its citation in *EPB*, and to be inclusive, rather than selective, of articles contained in a given issue of a journal. With the second volume in 1973, frequency of publication became bimonthly. Photoreplication of tables of contents was abandoned in favor of a greater readability and consistency in appearance. A new classification scheme was introduced to accommodate users of varying degrees of research sophistication and to enable specialists to review quickly the literature of their particular disciplines. Journals were classified into six broad categories: General/Human Ecology, Air, Energy, Land Resources, Water Resources, and Nutrition and Health. Tables of contents for journals were then gathered into sections corresponding to these categories so that a reader interested primarily in air or water could turn to the appropriate section and quickly scan the recently published article titles from major journals in that specialized field. Each article citation was numbered for easy reference.

The most significant change in the second volume was the addition of subject and author indexing in individual issues, with a cumulative annual index published as the final issue for each year. The decision was made that *every* author of record, including corporate authors, would be listed in the author index to each issue and the cumulated annual index. The 1973 year-end index cumulated citations to almost 25,000 articles from Volumes 1 and 2.

The subject indexing scheme for *EPB* had taken more than a year to create. Boehm, an experienced bibliographer and indexer, was well acquainted with the labor-intensive nature of bibliographic publishing, and had begun to experiment with ways in which the computer might substitute for some of the repetitious human tasks associated with indexing the huge volume of material being published on environmental topics. To make the *EPB* subject index truly useful for nonspecialists, as well as experts in the various disciplines represented, the indexing language had to be broad enough to allow a user to locate an article by searching under terms meaningful to him or her. For example, articles should be accessible through common as well as scientific names for species or chemicals on which they focused, by geographic descriptors, and by biographic descriptors.

To achieve this goal of ready accessibility, Boehm devised a computer-assisted indexing program called "SPIndex," for "Subject Profile Index." To create a SPIndex entry, trained editors select several key descriptors (usually from three to seven terms) for each article title included in an issue of *EPB*. Together these terms, which are derived either from the article title or from the body of the article, "profile" the contents of the article. A computer program then rotates the descriptors so that each appears in turn as the lead term in alphabetical sequence in the index, followed by the other terms, and by the article's numeric citation. This process is best shown by example. Those below are taken from a recent issue.[1]

from Table of Contents section:

Part 1. General. Human Ecology
1.1 Broad Interest and Public Concern Journals
Ambio/A Journal of the Human Environment (Sweden)
1988 Vol. XVII, No. 3
17:12924 Heavy metals and other non-oil pollutants in southeast Asia
M. Hungspreugs p. 178

from SPIndex, repeated in alphabetical sequence under each descriptor:

Heavy metal. Pollutant, non-oil. Southeast Asia. 12924

from Table of Contents section:

Part 2. Air
Atmospheric Environment
1988 Vol. 22, No. 5

17:14224 Some aspects of the distribution of polycyclic aromatic hydrocarbons (PAH) between particles and gas phase from diluted gasoline exhaust generated with the use of a dilution tunnel, and its validity for measurement in ambient air R. Westerholm, U. Stenberg, and T. Alsberg p.1005

from SPIndex, repeated in alphabetical sequence under each descriptor:

Air pollution research. Dilution tunnel. Gas phase. Gasoline exhaust. Hydrocarbon, polycyclic aromatic. Particle composition. 14224

from Table of Contents section:

Part 6. Nutrition and Health
Journal of Toxicology—Clinical Toxicology
1988 Vol. 26, No. 1—2
17-17179 Toxicokinetics of paraquat through the heart—lung block. Six cases of acute human poisoning F.J. Baud, P. Houze, C. Bismuth, J.-M. Scherrmann, A. Jaeger, and C. Keyes p.35

from SPIndex, repeated in alphabetical sequence under each descriptor:

Heart—lung. Paraquat. Plasma concentration. Poisoning, human, acute. Toxicokinetics. 17179

The classification and indexing schemes developed for *Environmental Periodicals Bibliography* Volume 2, 1973, continue to the present. The number of citations per volume has remained constant at approximately 25,000 since Volume 6, 1977. The indexing language is constantly refined to reflect current usage. Indexing has become more precise, and the original goal of total inclusiveness of table of contents listings has been modified slightly: now all articles with an environmental dimension are included in the table of contents listings. The objective of broad coverage of environmental topics and the representation of the full spectrum of environmental publications has continued. Roughly 350 international periodicals are now represented in *Environmental Periodicals Bibliography*.

Advisory Board Participates in Journal Selection

The process of journal selection is ongoing. In so dynamic a field as the environment new titles are constantly appearing and must be evaluated for inclusion. The editors, assisted by a board of 12 advisors from academia, industry, environmental organizations, research laboratories, government, and scientific and research libraries, routinely evaluate new publications and review those currently indexed in *EPB*.[2]

Criteria for selection include: relevance, a primary concentration on one or more facets of the environment; high quality of articles, editorial responsibility, a positive reputation within the discipline covered; availability of the journal, a pattern of regular and dependable publication. Other guiding principles in journal selection include balance in subject matter and viewpoint, ensuring that the array of environmental positions and concerns is represented, and good international representation. In general, journals may be classified as industrial, political, medical, technical, biological, or social in their orientation.

A complete list of periodicals covered appears in each issue of *EPB*.[3] The list is coded to indicate which of these titles is represented in the particular issue. The great majority of periodicals indexed in *EPB* are provided by their publishers at no charge, and a few are on an exchange basis. Lag time between receipt of journals in the editorial office and their citation in *EPB* is normally three months or less.

Despite the growth in coverage and the volume of material processed each year, the editorial staff responsible for creating *EPB* has remained small. The "person—computer" interface Boehm envisioned continues to function effectively, and he frequently refers to *EPB* as "to our knowledge, the most cost-effective bibliographic service extant."

Developed for Diverse Audience

The audience for which the publication is intended has always been broad, including academic libraries and their varied constituents, government agencies, researchers, consultants, lawyers and legislators, the general public, and—especially—corporations involved in causing, correcting, and preventing environmental pollution. While all entries are indexed in English (with the exception of Latin scientific names, proper names, and geographic descriptors), coverage is international and so is the audience to which the publication is directed. From the beginning, subscribers have been almost evenly divided between the United States and abroad, and between academic and other types of libraries, many of them special libraries in petroleum companies and large engineering and construction firms. The composition of the subscriber base has fluctuated dramatically over the years, reflecting the attitude of the federal government toward environmental issues, the level of funding of the Environmental Protection Agency and state agencies modeled on it, federal support of environmental research programs and conservation research, and the current level of petroleum prices and the state of international petroleum and natural gas exploration. The shift in recent years has been heavily toward academic library subscribers and away from government, industry, and corporate libraries.

The Role of Secondary Resources in the Current Library Climate

As periodical prices, especially in the sciences, challenge the ability of libraries to maintain vast collections, the role of secondary reference tools such as *Environmental Periodicals Bibliography* becomes increasingly significant. These services allow readers to be aware of currently published material from a large number of original sources, many of them too expensive or too limited in scope to be affordable by most libraries. Described by Eric Boehm as "First Echelon" bibliographic services, they "consist of a basic bibliography composed only of citations, without annotations. [They] should be enhanced by subject or index headings, as the *simplest and most economical device*[*s*] for aiding the user initially." (emphasis added)[4] Boehm envisioned this first echelon of bibliography as "inclusive, a listing of all books or articles with the necessary bibliographical citations . . . Knowledge of existence or location, or availability, is most important . . ."[5] Once the reader is aware of the existence of an article, he or she has the opportunity to seek additional information through a second echelon bibliographic service (i.e., an abstracting service specializing in the discipline of interest), to secure the original journal (e.g., by interlibrary loan), or to request a copy of the article from the original publisher or an article copying service.

Initial use of the first echelon service for screening current literature has enormous advantages in saving both time and money. No reader, specialist or generalist, can possibly keep track of all currently published material within a single, well-defined scientific or technical field, let alone within the wide-ranging disciplines comprising environmental studies. While it is no longer practical to read, or even browse through, all potentially relevant journals, virtually any reader, even an undergraduate with limited library research skills, can quickly scan important publications in a specialized field by turning to the appropriate table of contents section within *EPB*. That same reader can search for a specific topic of interest published in peripheral or even nonrelated fields by checking a few key words in SPIndex. A final review of the author index to locate recently published work by known specialists in the field can further ensure the interested reader of finding all relevant recent articles on his or her topic.

By maintaining a reference collection that includes a first echelon bibliographic service such as *EPB*, focused on international publications dealing with environmental topics, a library faced with a reduced or frozen periodicals budget can still offer readers an opportunity to learn about newly published material in periodicals outside the library's collection. These may include expensive foreign publications, highly specialized scientific or technical periodicals, or titles that are infrequently used. Secondary reference materials lend themselves to regional collection building, library consortia, and other forms of pooled resources that stretch library dollars and ensure quality service.

ADDITIONAL SERVICE

In 1976, the International Academy at Santa Barbara signed an agreement with Lockheed's DIALOG Information Service to make the *Environmental Periodicals Bibliography* database available online to subscribers to the DIALOG service. Despite the fact that the *EPB* database had been maintained on tape since the second volume, and notwithstanding the computer-assisted nature of the editorial process, the conversion proved to be complex and time-consuming. It was not until 1978 that users first had access to *Environmental Bibliography*, the machine readable version of the *EPB* database.

That file, available through DIALOG as File #68, currently contains more than 360,000 complete bibliographic records going back to 1973. In a single search, a user may locate the most recent article on a highly specialized research topic or may review the wealth of information detailing the complex histories of such topics as acid precipitation, global warming, or nuclear fallout. Online searching has proven to be a fast and economical means of accessing specific information within the huge body of environmental literature. For small libraries or those with limited demand for environmental information, it can be an effective alternative to a subscription. In larger academic libraries, and in corporate research libraries, it is usually seen as an adjunct to the hard copy file. Frequently it is the first resort in a search process, quickly determining whether new material exists on a specific topic and, if so, where it may be located.

To facilitate searching of the database, the International Academy publishes a search guide, now in its third edition. *Environmental Bibliography Search Guide* offers the user information on composition of the database, hints on searching the file, a copy of the "cues for indexers" that shows the conventions followed in this natural language index, including the treatment of compound words and phrases, a contents page from the hard copy publication defining categories and subcategories reflected in tables of contents, a list of periodicals covered, DIALOG users' notes, and, finally, a copy of the most recent cumulative annual index to *EPB*. This tool has proven popular, especially as end-users, rather than trained librarians, increasingly conduct online searches.

The *Environmental Bibliography* file on DIALOG may be accessed through Easynet, General Videotext, DELPHI, Mead Data

Central, Western Union Infomaster, OCLC LINK, and Research Libraries Information Network.

GEARING UP FOR SPECIAL INTEREST PUBLICATIONS

For almost two decades *EPB* has effectively served the information needs of those concerned with the environment. Among the plans for the future of the publication are improved accessibility and retrieval capabilities that will allow for highly specialized searches of the current and historic database and the production of small, spin-off bibliographies in hard copy and on disk.

REFERENCES

1. *Environmental Periodicals Bibliography*, Volume 17, No. 4, 1988.
2. A list of Advisory Board members appears on the inside cover of each issue of *Environmental Periodicals Bibliography*.
3. The International Academy at Santa Barbara will be pleased to provide a complete list of periodicals currently covered in *EPB*.
4. Boehm, Eric H. *Blueprint for bibliography*. Santa Barbara, California: Clio Press; 1965.
5. *op. cit.*

Bowker A & I Environment Database: Major Features and Editorial Policies

David J. Packer

The abstracting and indexing division of the R.R. Bowker Company was launched in May 1988 with the acquisition of eight sci-tech databases from EIC/Intelligence. All of the Bowker A & I databases—Acid Rain, Artificial Intelligence, Biotechnology, CAD/CAM, Energy, Environment, Robotics, and Telecommunications—offer access to varied levels of technical and popular information of concern to researchers, corporate strategists, students, lawyers, policymakers, and the interested public. The largest of these databases and the subject of this article is the Environment A & I Services. In existence since 1970, *Environment Abstracts* contains more than 130,000 records providing multidisciplinary coverage of scientific, technical, socioeconomic, and public policy issues in the environmental and natural resources literature. *Environment Abstracts* compiles, summarizes, and indexes contributions on such topics as air, water, and soil pollution, toxicology, land use and misuse, waste management, weather modification, and endangered species. This paper is intended to provide science librarians with insight into the composition of the database, including retrieval formats, subject and source coverage, indexing procedures, and search options. Much of this information is now available to our users as part of the expanded instructional material and special features in the "front matter" of the print services.

The A & I Environment Services consist of three retrieval for-

---

David J. Packer, PhD, is Senior Editor, Environment Group, Bowker A & I Publishing, 245 W. 17th St., New York, NY 10011.

The author would like to thank his editorial and marketing colleagues for the right to draw freely from journal and promotional materials, and the management of the R.R. Bowker Co. for permission to submit this paper.

© 1990 by The Haworth Press, Inc. All rights reserved.

mats. In addition to *Environment Abstracts*, which is a monthly journal of abstracts and indexes, there are hardbound annual cumulations, and for investigators who prefer computer searching, an online service called Enviroline. The annuals offer a fully-indexed, yearly cumulation of abstracts for convenient retrospective research together with some special features described below. The instant, universal retrieval capabilities of Enviroline are available through two major online vendors, DIALOG and ORBIT. All of the A & I databases will soon join Bowker's family of Plus System CD-ROM products. CD-ROM's immense storage capacity and myriad searching capabilities promise unprecedented user-friendly access to the complete database. Bowker's A & I Document Retrieval Service complements these formats with the ability to supply full-text microfiche or hardcopy of approximately 80 percent of each month's abstracted articles. Since CD-ROM, the online services and the annual cumulations all grow directly from production of the monthly *Environment Abstracts* journal, a description of general editorial procedures and guidelines follows from consideration of the print format.

In 1989 the number of abstracts and citations in the monthly journals was increased from 500 to an average of 550, while the number of issues was increased from ten to twelve. These changes were designed to maximize the currency of data in the face of a voluminous and growing literature, and to enhance the ability of the print journal to deliver current information in a convenient and timely package. Among the nearly five thousand sources screened for relevant literature are the major domestic and international serials that regularly contain articles selected for abstracting. These 350 or so "core" and "primary" scientific, technical, and trade journals are found in the journals listing in the introductory material of the print monthly. Approximately fifteen core journals are dedicated to environment issues, with at least 80 percent of their articles selected for abstracting. It may be worth emphasizing that environment issues as defined here refer to the impact of humankind and technology on the environment, which does not include the basic science literature on ecology and species adaptations.

Bowker also covers literature that is narrowly distributed and often difficult to obtain, including conference and seminar proceedings, edited volumes of original papers, government and association reports, and the so-called grey matter of advocacy newsletters. The distribution of the various sources and document types is about 40 percent research, journal, and newsletter articles, 30 percent conference papers, and 30 percent special reports. *Environment Abstracts* is primarily an English language database; foreign language articles lacking an English abstract are excluded. Because of the thousands of sources and the finite size of the monthly journal, the database is not an appropriate vehicle for dissemination of news information whose primary value is timeliness. The lag time between the arrival of a document at Bowker and its appearance in the database currently averages about three to five months. These constraints dictate that brief, non-analytical news reports of breaking events are generally not included in the database. However, subsequent feature articles that appear in general or special interest magazines or newsletters will be abstracted. This procedure has the advantage of minimizing redundancy, which is also avoided by seeking primary sources for articles on focal issues and emerging technologies. The screening of sources and selection of articles for abstracting is responsive to the need of investigators for a comprehensive list of references in a particular field rather than an editor's chosen sample.

Each article selected for abstracting can be placed into one of 21 Review Categories such as air pollution, land use and misuse, and radiological contamination. (A complete list of categories with descriptions is appended.) In turn, these broad subject categories represent the initial step in the indexing process. As a search option, abstracts in each of the Review Categories can be scanned to monitor the latest developments in a broad field of interest. Abstract quality is consistently high because an author's abstract is either revised or rewritten by our own staff of highly qualified abstractors. Each concise abstract (about 100 words) is preceded by full bibliographic information, including author and title of the article, name of publication, publication date, page number, article length, a note on figures and references, as well as an indication of full-text microfiche availability from Bowker. Every abstract receives a unique and sequential accession number which permits easy access from the indexes. These indexes provide the more specific search options.

Two of the indexes, author and source, are derived directly from the bibliographic data. Although a maximum of two authors appears in the bibliographic citations accompanying the abstract, the Author Index lists all authors together with the article's accession number. The Source Index lists the citation information and accession number under the name of the publication in which the article appeared. A third index and the most often used pathway to particular abstracts is the Subject Index. To create this index, the editors thoroughly characterize each database entry (abstract) by assigning keyterms according to established indexing guidelines. The keyterms or descriptors serve as headings in the Subject Index, and include general subject references and specific technical terminology, as well as the names of organizations, government agencies, laws, and geographic locations. Up to 14 separate keyterms are assigned to the articles in primary, secondary, and tertiary echelons. The three levels represent a descending order of specificity and exact relevance to the article. It is here that the number of access points differs among the three delivery formats. Only the primary terms (generally three to five per abstract) are available in the monthly journal, whereas Enviroline and the Annuals offer all three levels. (Prior to 1988, the annual Subject Index included only primary and secondary terms.) Nevertheless, primary terms are carefully selected for accuracy and completeness, while skimming the monthly abstracts by review category is analogous to the broadened search capabilities of the larger formats. Plans for a thesaurus complete with cross-referencing and a hierarchy structure will aid in all aspects of keyterm-based searches for the 1990 volume. An additional form of subject access, the Industry Index, further classifies articles describing the products or services of particular industries. Articles on scrap materials recycling are common entries here. Industry keyterms are drawn from the Standard Industrial Classification codes of the U.S. Department of Commerce. In sum, the Review Categories and four Indexes provide numerous pathways to specific articles in the print format. Eleven search categories are available on Enviroline, including abstract keyterms, review category, source publication and document type. Although the Enviroline User's Manual is currently out of print, customers should consult Bowker's Electronic Publishing Division for forthcoming availability. Keyterm lists are supplied upon request.

One special feature of the hardbound annual deserves mention.

The section entitled "The Year in Review" has been expanded for 1988 and subsequent years to include a legislative retrospective and two or more major review papers in different environmental fields. The review papers are contributed in most cases by members of a newly organized Board of Advisors. The hardbound annual provides a unique forum for such "annual reviews" by reaching a diverse audience of investigators in various subfields of the environmental sciences as well as decision-makers and non-professional users.

Our coverage of such core environmental topics as pollution, toxicology, and waste management is similar to competitive database products. However, many environmental studies, particularly those directed toward national and global management and policy issues, are multidisciplinary or interdisciplinary in scope. The 21 Review Categories of *Environment Abstracts* provide the broad view and organizational structure (including categories on international and U.S. policy issues) necessary to incorporate such studies and act as an information base for future studies. Furthermore, there is a growing recognition that human population pressure and overpopulation is an environmental issue. Category 13 of the review classification considers the physical and socioeconomic aspects of human population growth and control, while such categories as Land Use & Misuse, Oceans & Estuaries, and Solid Waste cover the potential environmental consequences of human subsistence activities. In terms of coverage and accessibility, the A & I Environment Database is a uniquely comprehensive reference source, although comprehensiveness is a goal that we are compelled to approach asymptotically in managing the enormous and diverse environmental literature.

APPENDIX
Review Categories

All documents acquired by Bowker A & I are logged into 21 review categories for quick location according to broad areas of interest.

01 Air Pollution

Includes air pollution aspects of: mobile and stationary sources, gases and particulates; acid rain; odors; aquatic and marine atmospheres; thermal air pollution; control technologies. For airborne trace elements and pesticides see 02 Chemical & Biological Contamination; for radiological air pollution see 14 Radiological Contamination; for weather modification aspects see 20 Weather Modification & Geophysical Change.

02 Chemical & Biological Contamination

Includes chemical and biological contamination aspects of air, land, organisms, water; plant and animal diseases; pests; agricultural chemicals; insecticides, fungicides, rodenticides, herbicides; industrial chemicals; actual or potential trace element contamination; toxicological effects; chemical and biological weapons. For marine oil spills see 12 Oceans & Estuaries; for biological contamination of drinking water see 16 Renewable Resources—Water; for freshwater pollution aspects of fertilizers, detergents, and oil spills see 19 Water Pollution.

03 Energy

Includes nontechnical aspects and general environmental impact of energy development and utilization. For specific pollution aspects see 01 Air Pollution, 02 Chemical & Biological Contamination, 09 Land Use & Misuse, 10 Noise Pollution, 12 Oceans & Estuaries, 14 Radiological Contamination, 17 Solid Waste, 19 Water Pollution, 20 Weather Modification & Geophysical Change. (For more detailed information on energy development and utilization see Energy Information Abstracts.)

04 Environmental Education

Includes philosophical and operational aspects of: curriculum planning and development; environmental study areas; adult and community programs.

05 Environmental Design & Urban Ecology
Includes building and nonbuilding aesthetic aspects of: landscape architecture; visual pollution; billboards, transmission lines; urban design, planning, renewal; city streets; new towns; ekistics. For rural and regional planning see 09 Land Use & Misuse.

06 Food & Drugs
Includes food supply aspects of commercial fisheries, aquaculture and mariculture, livestock, field crops; food processing; nutritional requirements; animal feed. For pollution damage to food see 01 Air Pollution, 02 Chemical & Biological Contamination, 12 Oceans & Estuaries, 14 Radiological Contamination, 19 Water Pollution; for birth control drugs see 13 Population Planning & Control.

07 General
Includes general aspects of: U.S. pollution and conservation problems; policy, planning, and programs of U.S. federal, state, and local governments, trade and professional associations, corporations, environmental organizations. For specific environmental issues see individual categories.

08 International
Includes general aspects of non-U.S. and international pollution and conservation problems. For food supply aspects see 06 Food & Drugs; for marine aspects see 12 Oceans & Estuaries; for population aspects see 13 Population Planning & Control; for specific environmental issues see individual categories.

09 Land Use & Misuse
Includes use and despoilation of land and wetlands; subdivisions, construction, pipeline transmission, highway and airport development, stripmining; land reclamation; open space; wilderness; scenic and historic preservation; rural and regional planning; land-based recreation. For soil pollution see 02 Chemical & Biological Contamination; for terrestrial power plant siting see 03 Energy; for offshore power plant siting see 12 Oceans & Estuaries; for seismological considerations in power plant siting see 20 Weather Modification & Geophysical Change; for aesthetic aspects see 05 Environmental Design & Urban Ecology; for resource aspects of forest and wilderness see 15 Renewable Resources—Terrestrial; for waste disposal on land see 17 Solid Waste; for transportation aspects of highways and airports see 18 Transportation; for game preserves see 21 Wildlife.

10 Noise Pollution
Includes noise levels and effects from domestic, industrial, and transportation sources.

11 Non-Renewable Resources
Includes resource aspects of minerals. For scenic aspects see 09 Land Use & Misuse; for recycling see 17 Solid Waste.

12 Oceans & Estuaries
Includes use and abuse of marine environment; international agreements on seabed usage; technology and programs for exploitation; ocean mining, artificial structures, offshore power plant siting; marine pollution; ocean dumping, marine oil spills, sewage outfalls, thermal marine pollution; oceanography. For pollution of marine atmosphere see 01 Air Pollution; for marineborne trace elements and pesticides see 02 Chemical & Biological Contamination; for mariculture see 06 Food & Drugs; for radiological marine pollution see 14 Radiological Contamination; for freshwater pollution see 19 Water Pollution.

13 Population Planning & Control
Includes physical, psychological, and socioeconomic aspects of human population growth and control; incentives and regulations; birth control programs and techniques, contraception, sterilization , abortion. For population support aspects of food supply see 06 Food & Drugs.

14 Radiological Contamination
Includes radiation levels and effects from: atomic and electromagnetic sources; lab and mine accidents; waste disposal; fallout; nuclear fuel and reactor safety. For energy aspects of atomic reactors see 03 Energy.

15 Renewable Resources—Terrestrial
Includes renewable aspects of plants and soil; forest management; tree farms, logging, reforestation; soil conservation; botany. For soil pollution see 02 Chemical & Biological Contamination; for land use aspects see 09 Land Use & Misuse.

16 Renewable Resources—Water
Includes renewable aspects of fresh water; water supply; water resources, water purification, desalination, irrigation, biological contamination of drinking water; flood control; artificial lakes; water-based recreation. For aquaculture see 06 Food & Drugs; for marine resources see 12 Oceans & Estuaries; for pollution aspects and wastewater treatment see 19 Water Pollution.

17 Solid Waste

Includes solid waste handling, treatment technologies, disposal; municipal and industrial refuse; sanitary landfill, compaction, composting, incineration; recycling; hazardous waste treatment and containment; land disposal of liquid wastes. For air contamination aspects see 01 Air Pollution; for ocean dumping see 12 Oceans & Estuaries; for radioactive waste disposal see 14 Radiological Contamination.

18 Transportation

Includes transportation aspects of: motor vehicles and highways, aircraft and airports, railroads, ships, mass transit; pipeline transportation; new concepts; magnetic levitation, personal rapid transit. For pollution aspects see 01 Air Pollution, 10 Noise Pollution, 12 Oceans & Estuaries, 14 Radiological Contamination, 17 Solid Waste, 19 Water Pollution, 20 Weather Modification & Geophysical Change; for urban aspects see 05 Environmental Design & Urban Ecology; for nonurban land use aspects see 09 Land Use & Misuse.

19 Water Pollution

Includes freshwater pollution aspects of agriculture effluents; fertilizers, animal wastes; industrial effluents; wastewater, thermal water pollution; municipal effluents; sewage, detergents, freshwater oil spills; wastewater treatment and reuse. For pollution of aquatic atmospheres see 01 Air Pollution; for waterborne trace elements and pesticides see 02 Chemical & Biological Contamination; for marine pollution see 12 Oceans & Estuaries; for radiological water pollution see 14 Radiological Contamination; for land disposal of liquid wastes see 17 Solid Waste.

20 Weather Modification & Geophysical Change

Includes geophysical impact of use of environmental resources; unintentional and deliberate weather modification; thermal pockets, greenhouse effect, ozone depletion, geophysical warfare; nuclear winter; earthquakes; seismological considerations in power plant siting. For ozone pollution and acid rain see 01 Air Pollution.

21 Wildlife

Includes wildlife aspects of animal habitat; endangered species; game preserves; bird sanctuaries; predator control; ichthyology. For pollution effects on nonendangered species see 01 Air Pollution, 02 Chemical & Biological Contamination, 10 Noise Pollution, 12 Oceans & Estuaries, 14 Radiological Contamination, 19 Water Pollution; for livestock see 06 Food & Drugs.

Reprinted with permission of R. R. Bowker, 245 W. 17th Street, New York, N.Y. 10011.

SPECIAL PAPER

Computer Searching of Chemical Databases by Faculty and Students at the University of Rochester

Arleen N. Somerville

SUMMARY. Since 1979 senior chemistry majors at the University of Rochester have learned to search chemical databases online. In 1984 this instruction was extended to faculty, graduate students and other research staff in several University departments. This article discusses the promotion, objectives, teaching techniques, logistics, and impact of the program.

INTRODUCTION

The University of Rochester is an academically selective private institution with nationally recognized undergraduate and doctoral programs in the sciences, with special strength in chemistry. The Department of Chemistry offers rigorous B.A. and B.S. curricula for its majors. All majors take 12 credits of organic chemistry as sophomores, including an organic laboratory sequence, which in the spring semester introduces the students to the original scientific

---

Arleen N. Somerville is Head of the Science and Engineering Libraries, as well as the Chemistry Librarian, at the University of Rochester. She received her BS and MLS from the University of Wisconsin at Madison.

© 1990 by The Haworth Press, Inc. All rights reserved.

literature in the planning and execution of an experiment and in the identification of an unknown compound. In the junior and senior years the program introduces the student to independent study and research. Thus the junior year lab offers advanced analytical, physical and synthetic techniques characteristic of the main areas of chemistry. All B.S. and many B.A. candidates do independent research in their senior year under guidance of a faculty member. The B.S. program, completed by 10-20 students per year, is designed to educate the student as a professional chemist or to do graduate work in chemistry or biochemistry.

The strong and rigorous undergraduate chemistry curriculum is matched by the high quality graduate and post-doctoral teaching and research programs. In 1988/89 the Chemistry Department had 25 faculty, 130 graduate students, and 20 post-doctoral fellows, and about $5 million dollars of external research funding. In December 1988 the Department was selected as the site of one of 11 newly designated National Science Foundation Science and Technology Centers. Overall, the Department ranks ninth in the country for federal research funding per faculty member, with internationally recognized strengths in organic synthesis, photochemistry, inorganic-organometallic chemistry, chemical physics, and nuclear physics.

Significant chemical research is also conducted by researchers in the Pharmacology and Biophysics Departments at the Medical Center in such areas as drug synthesis and metabolism, metabolic deactivation of xenobiotics, and magnetic resonance imaging. Several chemists support the laser fusion research of the Laboratory for Laser Energetics. Chemical engineering research and teaching programs cover polymers, surface chemistry, catalysis, systems and control, energy resources, environmental engineering, and computer applications.

PROMOTION

Undergraduate Students

Teaching chemistry seniors to search computerized databases is part of an extensive information instruction program which is integrated into a variety of courses. This program began in 1979 with implementation of a National Science Foundation grant.[1] Faculty and students participated in discussions that helped form the instruction program. Their ideas grew from experiences with pre-1979 information instruction classes. The Chemistry Department Chairman had previously paid for a new 1200 baud terminal and agreed to help support the program financially at the end of the two-year grant. This early involvement of faculty and students, along with the librarian's already-established credibility, helped ensure initial and continuing support from the Chemistry Department. While all other instruction is integrated into relevant courses, computer searching is treated as a special topic and taught outside regular classes during the month of September. This usually means classes are held during evenings or Saturday afternoons. Letters, with return post cards, are sent to each chemistry major during the spring or summer prior to their senior year. Signed by both the chemistry librarian and an organic chemistry professor, the letter describes the opportunity to learn computer searching, stresses the value for their professional careers, and indicates the time and location of the first meeting. Completing this instruction in September helps students use computer searching needed for senior research and avoids overloading their already demanding schedules once lab reports and examinations begin in early October.

Researchers

Since 1975 when computer searching was introduced, chemistry faculty, post-doctoral fellows, and graduate students have been among the most frequent requesters of searches. The chemistry librarian lectures frequently in graduate courses in which she discusses how to find information efficiently that is needed for that course. The information might be used in writing a paper or in answering questions that arise in lab work. These lectures are followed by a practice questions assignment, except when paper writing provides practice opportunities, and are graded by the librarian.

Consciousness-raising lectures titled "How Computer Searching Can Aid Chemical Research" are delivered to various research groups during their weekly group meetings. Such lectures offer opportunities to select questions related to the group's subject interests and to use a professor from the group for the author and citation question examples. Such targeted presentations are effective in arousing interest and enthusiasm. This interest makes it easy to incorporate information about related databases and systems and produces greater understanding of the value of computer searching.[2]

The extensive information instruction activity by the chemistry librarian laid a firm base for extending computer search training to researchers. This was done in 1984 when the Academic Plan for Chemical Abstracts Service (CAS) files was offered by STN International. The initial memo offering the mini-course was sent to each chemistry professor and, at the suggestion of the Chemistry Department Chairman, to several faculty in the Pharmacology Department of the Medical Center. Subsequently, inquiries were received from researchers in other chemically-oriented Medical Center departments, the Chemical Engineering Department, and the laboratory for Laser Energetics. Prior to each instruction unit, a memo is sent to all faculty in relevant research areas and active liaison representatives informing them of the upcoming classes, specifying the cost, and requesting schedule information. All interested attendees are accommodated.

OBJECTIVES

Undergraduates

The objectives for undergraduates are to teach:

1. both the benefits and limitations of computer searching;
2. when a computer search is an appropriate way to answer a question;
3. how to develop an effective search strategy; and
4. how to conduct a computer search.

Additional objectives include learning:

1. to recognize librarians as technically informed consultants, and
2. how to be effective users of academic and industrial libraries.

Researchers

The same objectives apply to researchers as to undergraduates. An additional objective for researchers is to teach them to search effectively and efficiently. Therefore, greater attention is given to online problem solving.

Several professors have indicated that they consider it important that each graduate student learn to conduct structure and bibliographic searches. Training is considered essential. Computer search training is considered as important as instrumentation training.

TEACHING TECHNIQUES

Many teaching techniques are common to all computer search instruction. A sample search demonstration begins the first lecture and serves to pique their interest, ensures that all attendees realize what they will be striving to achieve, and offers an opportunity to define contents of a computer record. A question relevant to the group's interest is best, but if time is not available to develop this question or if the interests are diverse, a question selected from the CINF module can be used. Information jargon is avoided, unless it's essential to know.

Introductory manuals were developed in-house for bibliographic and structure searching.[3] These manuals focus on the commands and search techniques needed most often by chemists.[4] The manuals refer to page numbers in the vendor documentation, so the attendees can easily read more detailed information as needed. The typical and most important questions, as well as efficient ways to search these questions, are specified. Among the questions included are: synthesis of a substance, properties of a substance, review articles, and authors' publications. System commands are largely taught in the context of answering these questions. The instructions demonstrate all steps needed to answer a question instead of relying on application of instructions from disparate sections of documentation. For example, modifying a structure in a structure search may require deleting nodes and bonds, connecting different nodes, and assigning new bond values. These steps are stated explicitly. Tailoring instruction to the group's needs facilitates learning and adds to the instructor's credibility. Such an approach also avoids overwhelming chemists with unnecessary detail, but still permits emphasizing that careful preparation and knowledge of database organization and contents are crucial to success. This targeted instruction to meet the group's information needs is extremely time-consuming but is usually more effective.[5]

The same manuals are used for both undergraduates and researchers. However, the lectures presented to researchers include greater emphasis on indexing policies and efficient search techniques.

Two group lectures introduce each of the two topics—bibliographic and structure searching. Each lecture is approximately 3/4-1 1/2 hours and scheduled whenever the attendees have time available during the day, in the evenings, or on Saturdays. The lectures are typically scheduled approximately two weeks apart. This allows time for each attendee to schedule a practice session before the second lecture, while not delaying the followup lecture so long that information would be forgotten.

An online practice session is scheduled after each lecture for all attendees. Learning files, with questions provided in workbooks, are available from several vendors.[6] These files are adequate to teach basic search mechanics and database organization. Practice questions are provided for undergraduates, although each is asked to bring his/her own question to the second practice session. The questions used for the second session include a question that asks the students to locate articles by Department faculty on their research specialties. The students can choose among six faculty from inorganic, organic, and physical chemistry, so they usually can select a favorite professor. The assigned questions also reflect subject areas of interest in the Department research laboratories and include, for example, laser temperature jump studies, nmr of polynucleotides, synthesis of daunomycin, and resonance Raman spectra of hemoglobin. Researchers, on the other hand, bring their own questions from the laboratory to the practice sessions. This provides incentive to "get into it." They are encouraged to do typical kinds of searches, such as synthesis, properties, author, author on a specific subject, restriction to specific time periods, etc.

TEACHING CHEMICAL ABSTRACTS

The first lecture covers basic search mechanics, some subject searching, some substance searching (for researchers only), an in-depth look at the Basic Index, and techniques for developing a search strategy. The first lecture begins with a sample search. Then, a schematic diagram is discussed that shows the progression from an author to a journal, etc., to the database producer, to a vendor, to the searcher. This diagram, included as an Appendix in the manual, helps attendees understand the difference between a database and a vendor, as well as to recognize where the computer is located that they are searching. Another diagram, also an Appendix in the manual, depicts the major chemistry databases offered by the vendor. In this case, it is Chemical Abstracts Services' databases on STN International.

The six steps in computer searching are covered on the first two pages of the manual: logging in, selecting a file, searching, combining answer numbers and terms, displaying records, and logging off. The Boolean operators (AND, OR, NOT) are discussed in the searching step. At that point it is appropriate to describe the search process, so that attendees recognize that the computer system searches the entire database for each term typed before the Boolean operation occurs. The combining of answer numbers and search terms is demonstrated by using a wide variety of examples. The crucial need to group terms with the same Boolean operator when using both AND and OR is stressed. One example provides an excellent demonstration of disastrous results if parentheses are not used to group terms. A general format for displaying references is provided, as well as definitions for each format, and specific examples, such as

General formula:

DIS L# format-name(s) no. of references
    (1)   (2)   (3)

Examples:

DIS L4 CBIB 1-4,6,8-10 (CBIB format for document nos. 1-4,6,8-10 from answer No. L4).[7]

The last-in, first-out principle is described.

Two special ways for searching, truncation and the wild card character, are described in the manual.

1. Truncation: search on a root or stem of a word. (CA File, p.16)
   There are two symbols for truncation:
   ? use at the end of a term to represent zero or any number of characters

   Example:
   spectr? = spectra
   spectrometry
   spectroscopy
   spectrum

   # use at the end of a term to represent zero or one character. This is useful for plurals formed by adding an "s".
   Example:
   laser# = laser
   lasers

2. "Wild Card" character (CA File, p. 16)
   Symbol is ! It can be used within a term or at the end of a term.

   Example:

   synthes!s = synthesis
   syntheses[8]

The importance of not truncating to an excessively short root is stressed and demonstrated with a humorous, but chemical example (spec = spectra, speckled trout, etc.).

Proximity searching is defined and offered as a way of searching more precisely. The operators defined with examples include: (W), (nW), (A), (nA), (L).

Proximity Operators: specify that search terms and answer nos. appear in specified relationships to each other (CA File, p. 25-33).

Operators	Values	Examples
(w)	adjacent, in order specified	nuclear(w)magnetic
(nw)	n or fewer words apart, in order specified	heat (lw)fusion
(A)	adjacent, in any order	shale(A)oil
(nA)	n or fewer words apart, in any order	air(1A)pollution
(L)	words or registry numbers occur in same information unit, e.g., title, keyword phrase, or single index heading-text modification combination; the words or registry nos. could be represented by an answer no.[9]	50-00-0(L)synthes!s 50-00-0(L) (IR or infrared) photolysis(L)porphyrin? 50-00-0(L)L5 L2(L)L8

Information found in the Basic Index fields is described in detail. The printed counterpart of each field is noted, which helps end users relate to the material. For CA searching it is important to stress that information matching the search criteria could appear in any one or more fields in the Basic Index. It can be difficult to predict this, so it is important to determine how each search concept would appear in each part of the Basic Index. Table 1 shows the type of access terms found in each field of the Basic Index.[10]

The importance of using abbreviations found in keywords and modifying phrases is demonstrated by a search for references on oxidation of methane (Reg. No. = 50-0-0):

    s oxidation (L) 50-00-0
        92260 OXIDATION
        17468 50-00-0

                3 OXIDATION (L) 50-00-0
      s (oxidation or oxidn) (L) (50-00-0)
         92260 OXIDATION
         135406 OXIDN
         17468 50-00-0
            824 (OXIDATION OR OXIDN) (L) (50-00-0)

A total of 821 of the 824 references would be missed if the abbreviation was omitted. This negative example can be much more effective than only demonstrating the correct method.

The steps for developing search strategy are followed as the class completes the strategy for searching the topic: Use of gas-liquid chromatography to analyze for such trace metals as mercury and lead.

Steps for Developing Search Strategy:

1. Determine the main subject concepts.
2. Determine the different ways of expressing each concept: consider each searchable part of the record. (Table 1)
3. Determine how to connect the terms, i.e., with the Boolean OR, AND, NOT.
4. Anticipate problems:
    a. if you get too many references, how will you narrow the search criteria.
    b. if you get too few references, how will you broaden the search criteria.
5. Write out the search strategy so you know exactly what you plan to do after beginning the search.
6. Begin searching.
7. After completing the last combination, check a few bibliographic records for relevancy and at least one complete record for additional search terms.
8. Alter search strategy, as needed.
9. Display relevant references.[11]

Because researchers' questions in the first practice session often involve chemical substances, their first lecture covers introductory comments about searching for substances. The focus is on search-

TABLE 1[10]

Examination of a Record: Subject Searching

All parts of the record reviewed here are searched <u>simultaneously</u> and is known as the Basic Index (BI).

Part of Record

Access Terms

Title of article (TI)
- Words used by chemists to describe subject.
  - Can be narrow or general
  - Compounds: common names, categories of compounds
  - New terms
  - Acronyms
  - Colloquial terms

Keywords (KW)
Key concepts of article; in back of current issues of CA
- Abbreviations
- Acronyms
- New terms
- Words that describe main topics of article
- Words that describe type of article, e.g., review
- Categories of compounds

General Subject Index (IT)
1. Main subject heading. From Index Guide.
2. Modifying phrases Any terms that further describe that topic.

1. Main heading
   - Limited to the phrases in the General Subject Index.
   - Complete words and phrases, e.g., Nuclear magnetic resonance.
2. Modifying phrases
   - Abbreviations
   - Common names of compounds
   - Acronyms
   - Words that more exactly describe the topic.
     - Narrow terms
     - General terms
     - New terms
     - Singular and plural words
     - Colloquial terms

Chemical Substance Index (IT)
1. Substance's Registry No.

1. Substance's Registry No.
   - The CAS index name is <u>not</u> in the record.
   - Includes EVERY substance of importance (e.g., product, starting material; property or process described); excludes most solvents, reagents, and some intermediates prior to 1985.

2. Modifying phrases

2. Modifying phrases
   Same characteristics as for the General Subject Index terms.

ing by Registry Number. The importance of doing so is reinforced by looking again at the complete record from the sample search. Major sources for finding registry numbers are described, e.g.:

- CA Index Guide;
- CA Registry File;
- CA Chemical Substance Index;
- Aldrich Catalog;
- Merck Index;
- Dictionary of Organic Compounds (DOC);
- Dictionary of Organometallic Compounds;
- Heilbron File (online) of DOC & Dictionary of Organometallic Compounds.

Ways to search the Registry File by molecular formula, common names, and name fragments are described very briefly. The first lecture is concluded with each participant scheduling a practice session.

The second lecture for both undergraduates and researchers begins with a brief discussion of the practice experiences. The instructor's comments reflect the group's experiences and usually include such topics as searching aspects that were handled well, reiteration of the need to use abbreviations and importance of viewing indexing for additional search terms, the importance of using (L), and the value of getting one answer number for each major concept. While end users may be reluctant to share experience, they can often be encouraged to participate when examples from their searches are mentioned by the instructor. This occurred, for example, while discussing the importance of identifying the need to use poly(L) nucleotides and c(L) glycosides, in addition to polynucleotides and c(w) glycosides. Another such drawing out of an attendee's comments occurred in discussing use of (L) rather than AND when searching for reduction of a substance to ensure the desired substance is the one undergoing reduction. This discussion also covers the system's treatment of punctuation marks, with x-ray as the typical example.

The lecture begins with author searching. The ease and speed with which an author's publications can be searched is contrasted to the much slower use of printed indexes. A transparency showing entries from the Author Index reminds attendees of printed index searches and provides a sharp contrast with rapid online author searching. The need to expand an author name and use /au to search the author field is demonstrated with a local chemistry professor's name.

The use and value of searching CA Section names and numbers is demonstrated. Searching for review articles is shown.

The value of searching in the CA abstract is discussed. This includes a review of the fields in the Basic Index. Search examples demonstrate the required parentheses to enclose multi-word search terms, e.g.,

S adriamycin/bi,ab
S (cytochrome (w)C)/bi,ab
S ((nmr or nuclear(w)magnetic(w)resonance) and (cytochrome(w)c or 9007-43-6))/bi,ab.[12]

Ways of overcoming "Truncation Limits Exceeded" and "System Limits Exceeded" messages are demonstrated.

Considerable time is spent discussing how to search for chemical substances. For undergraduates, searching by Registry Number is described. The same information covered in the first lecture to researchers is reviewed briefly. Searching by name fragments is discussed in greater detail. Salts can be difficult to locate, so Chemical Abstracts Service's naming practices and search techniques are described. Two pitfalls encountered with Registry Numbers are noted: existence of deleted and replaced Registry Numbers in the computer record, and use of unique Registry Numbers for each isomer and unspecified substance. CA indexing policies for substances that affect information searchable in the computer record are noted.[13] Searching substances by name or acronym is shown, along with a description of advantages and disadvantages. A search technique that ensures comprehensive coverage is provided:

General format: Registry Nos. OR common name/acronym.

Example: 50-00-0 or methane[14]

Preparation of a substance is a common question. Effective strategies are provided:

General format: Registry No.P (P = preparation)

Examples: 50-00-0P
16234-96-1P or (aklavinone or 16234-96-1) (L)synthes!s
Note: natural products require the additional link to synthesis.[15]

Properties of a substance is another typical question. Effective strategies are provided:

(trimethylphospane(w)oxide or 676-96-0) (L) (IR or infrared) to ensure IR of *this* oxide

OR

(trimethylphospane(w)oxide or 676-96-0) AND (IR or infrared)[16]

if comprehensive coverage is required and it doesn't matter if some irrelevant references are found.

Restricting a search to time periods stresses use of the RANGE command. The use of this command is demonstrated with search terms and answer numbers. The option of setting the RANGE at the beginning of a search is shown. How to save searches and answers on a temporary or long-term basis for future use is demonstrated, as well as how to re-use and delete saved searches.

Ways to improve search strategies are stressed for researchers. Efficient ways are provided for displaying the indexing of a good reference. This is followed by three ways to improve searches. Less effective search strategies can usually be improved by broadening or restricting the search or by reducing irrelevant references. Suggestions for broadening the search specific to searching CA include, for example,

- verifying that all necessary abbreviations, acronyms, and truncated words are used;
- limiting the search to fewer answer sets;
- evaluating the effectiveness of proximity operators:
  - should (L) be used rather than (w)
  - should (A) be used rather than (w)
  - should AND be used rather than (L)

- incorporating broader terms, e.g., iodinat? in addition to iodo?;
- using all relevant registry nos.[17]

Suggested ways to restrict a search include, for example,

- by year, using RANGE = ( );
- identifying review articles;
- adding additional search terms, e.g., a section code or narrow subject term;
- omitting more general items.[18]

Suggested ways to reduce irrelevant references include, for example,

- identifying terms that can be *added* to the search strategy, e.g.,
  - adding one or more CA sections or section groupings;
  - adding another subject concept;
- identifying terms that can be *eliminated* without losing valuable references, e.g.,
  - deleting one or more CA sections
  - identifying general terms that represent groups of references and using NOT to delete the references.[19]

It is useful to caution new searchers that it may be impossible to eliminate all irrelevant references without losing relevant ones because of the literalness of computer searching. It is wise to recognize when it is counterproductive or not cost effective to continue to refine search results. The value of reviewing the indexing of some irrelevant references to aid refinement of the search is mentioned. Chemical examples are used in highlighting the most valuable problem-solving techniques for refining search strategy.

Other search capabilities described briefly include:

- staying up-to-date (current awareness);
- requesting offline prints;
- searching by organization name, geographic location, and country;

- searching by journal name or CODEN;
- searching by type of publication, e.g., patent, book, dissertation;
- searching by language;
- using Display History command;
- using Set command to specify search parameters at beginning of search;
- displaying all or parts of the computer record when the CHEMICAL ABSTRACTS volume and abstract numbers are known.

Appendices include: graphical overview of the CAS databases on STN International; Boolean operators; abbreviations used by CHEMICAL ABSTRACTS; sample records showing the BIB, CBIB, and ALL formats from the CA File and the SUB format from the Registry File; name and formula search options for finding Registry Numbers in the Registry File; name segments searchable in the Registry File; and sources for search assistance, which list the librarian as the first source and the Search Assistance Desk as the second source.

The CA search segment of the lecture is completed with a review of the costs of searching CA File and the Registry File by name and formula-related options. The remainder of the lecture covers other databases and systems, search options in the library and their labs, software, and how to establish STN accounts.

The STN International database brochure is used to discuss the value of the other databases and to specify which are included in the Academic Plan. A continuously updated list of computerized databases in chemistry is distributed with comments about the most relevant ones. This also offers an opportunity to point out the other vendors and indicate which databases are searchable by using less expensive versions of the basic system.

A handout of the DIALOG subject groupings of databases demonstrates the wide diversity of available databases. A cited article search from the Science Citation Index is demonstrated. In the future, this will be augmented with information about the CD-ROM version, which was acquired during the writing of this article. The patent databases are highlighted, with comments about the other vendors who offer patent files. Brief comments are made about physics, biological, polymer, and medical databases of potential interest to attendees. A handout of BRS databases is used for highlighting several files, especially those searchable via BRS After-Dark or BRS Colleague.

After a discussion of search facilities in the library and their labs, the librarian's consultant role, and how to acquire passwords, each attendee signs up for the second practice search.

TEACHING SUBSTRUCTURE SEARCHING

Researchers from the Chemistry Department, Laser Lab, and the Pharmacology and Biophysics Departments of the Medical Center attend the substructure searching instruction, which is scheduled once or twice a year. All interested participants are accommodated, so class size varies from 12-20.

The two lectures each require 1 1/2-2 hours and each lecture is followed by a tutored practice session. A sample substructure search is demonstrated that identifies all substances with the following partial structure:[20]

FIGURE 1

R is not specified

A graphic overview of the CAS databases is useful to help attendees see how the Registry File fits into the overall picture. While attendees are encouraged to learn to search *Chemical Abstracts* first, that doesn't always occur, so this overview is especially important for those individuals.

A manual developed by the author, in consultation with a synthetic organic chemist, focuses on search techniques required to answer typical structure questions.

An important feature of the manual is the one-page Overview

which identifies the three major steps (STRUCTURE, SEARCH, DISPLAY) and commands that are required to complete the search. This Overview answers the question: What do I do next? See Table 2.

The manual follows the search process. How to graph rings is demonstrated with the GRAPH command. The numbering of the nodes assigned by the computer is specified for each example.

GRAPH R66   To create

GRAPH R8   To create[22]

FIGURE 2

As is true throughout the manual, the command to create chains is represented in a generalized format with an example of that format. For example:

Chain (C): x Cy (x = # of node; y = # of atoms in chain)

GRAPH 6 C1, 4 C3

to create

Nodes are numbered in the order they were created.[23]

FIGURE 3

Bridged and spiro ring systems occur sufficiently often in our searches that the commands for creating the bridged and spiro chains and rings are demonstrated.

Specifying nodes is covered in some detail. Again, the general format is specified, along with examples.

General format:

NODE x y (x = # of node, y = non-carbon atoms)
NODE x y, x x x y

Examples:

NODE 7 S
NODE 7 S, 10 13 16 N[24]

Other instructions cover valid element symbols, general symbols (i.e., x = any halogen), shortcut symbols (listed in an Appendix), negation of an element, variable nodes, and repeating groups. A note states that changing a node designation is done by respecifying the node.

Specifying BOND values is a crucial step, so emphasis on this occurs several times in the manual. BOND definitions are listed, as well as the generalized format and several examples. In addition to the typical examples, special shortcuts are noted, such as:

BOND ALL cs (all or almost all BOND values are the same, in this case chain single)
Note: can use when a few other bonds exist as well; just specify the others

For example: BOND All cs, 2-7 5-8 cd[25]

How to change a bond is specified, so there is no uncertainty. The manual notes that a BOND is changed by respecifying the value, i.e., BOND 1-2 cd (changed from cde).[26] The definition of tautomers is provided in detail and the importance of understanding the Chemical Abstracts Service use of tautomers for successful searches is stressed. The automatic detection and accommodation of tautomers with STN Express[27] is mentioned.

Table 2[21]

Overview

I. STRUCTURE (Command used to begin building structure)

Operation	Command
A. Build basic structure:	GRAPH
1. Ring structure	
2. Side chains	
B. Specify non-carbon atoms	NODE
C. Specify bonds	BOND
D. Specify attributes (Optional: Use as needed)	HCount Ring SPECification Node SPECification
E. Specify that structure building is complete:	END

Assigned an "L" answer no.

II. SEARCH (Command used to begin searching)

Operation (Answer questions)

1. Enter logic expression or query name (end): L#

2. Enter type of search: (SSS), family, exact: EXACT (IV-3, IV-17, IV-32)

3. Scope of search: (sample), full or range: SAMPLE

4. Search occurs. (Indicates the no. of iterations and answers in Sample Search, no. of projected iterations and answers, and likelihood of completion in the Full File.)

5. DISPLAY answers to sample search (if available)

NEXT: Change structure if necessary or complete search in Full File. Repeat same SEARCH steps as above, but specify FULL for Scope of Search.

III. DISPLAY References

Alternative 1	Alternative 2
Display references in the Registry File.	"Cross-over" to File CA to locate reference.)

The three ATTRIBUTES used most frequently are demonstrated: Hydrogen count, ring specification, and node specification. Formats are provided, along with comments on how and when to use them. The remaining attributes are listed with references to the full documentation.

How to DISPLAY Answers to substance searches and to bibliographic information is described in some detail. Use of the SELECT command to collect in one answer number those structures relevant for cross-over to CA File is demonstrated.

Ways to modify or correct structures are demonstrated. The DELETE commands for altering attributes, nodes, chains, rings, and bonds are shown. How to reconstruct a structure following deletion of a bond or node, etc. is specifically demonstrated. For example, the need to use the GRAPH command to create a new bond is shown and leaves no question about the appropriate next step. Use of a Registry Number as model for building a desired structure is discussed.

The first lecture concludes with all attendees signing up for a practice search.

The second lecture is shorter than the first and focuses on problem-solving. As is done in the second CA lecture, the lecturer makes observations from the practice searches and adds other relevant comments. Participants tend to be more willing to share experiences from the structure searching practice sessions than from bibliographic searching.

The critical step of identifying the appropriate substructure can often be a problem. The following list of suggestions for identifying substances was developed to help attendees develop a "feel" for specifying appropriate substructures.

1. General questions to ask:
   a. Why searching?
   b. What do I want to find?
   c. What do I want to exclude?

2. Specific questions to ask:
   a. What part of structure is most important to find information about?
      This question will help isolate the core of the question.
   b. In what structures could that core part be included?
   c. Define substructure to encompass all necessary contexts of the core part.
   d. Have I tried to eliminate potential irrelevant structures?
   e. Have I used HCo intelligently to eliminate unwanted answers, while retaining all answers of interest?

f. Have I been sufficiently specific to get a reasonable number of answers?

g. Have I identified ways of modifying the structure if I get too many iterations or answers, or too few? Have I identified alternative search strategies, such as using screens for simple substructures?

3. Keep a balance between specificity and generality.

Aid comes from judgment gained from experience and utilizing sample searches.

The discussion naturally leads to the Troubleshooting section of the manual. Attendees' experiences with Hydrogen Count use and encounters with tautomers are discussed using the manual's cautions and practice search examples. The importance of using the RC node specification to ensure retrieval as either a ring or chain is stressed. Iteration numbers greater than 20,000 occur frequently, so ways to decrease the number of iterations, beyond revision of the structure, focus on use of screens to eliminate irrelevant substances and to specify simple substructures (e.g., Hydrogen Augmented Atoms screens) and ways to restrict to desired substances. The option to divide a question into 2-3 segments is noted, with the caution to first call the Search Assistance Desk.

In order to search more precisely, the options for specifying the number of connections to an atom and the type of bond connections is described. For example, designation of the number of connections to a sulfur atom will produce substances containing S but not SO or SO_2. Ways to search several structures in one search refer to use of variable nodes and use of Boolean OR, along with the caution of the 20,000 iteration limit. The SAVE, SAVE TEMP and ACTIVATE options for re-using queries and answer numbers are described.

The Registry File segment of the lecture is concluded with a review of costs for EXACT, FAMILY, and SUBSTRUCTURE searches.

Other structure search databases are described and demonstrated. Searching the recently acquired SANDRA[28] (the floppy disk program that locates structures in the printed Beilstein volumes) and the computer searchable file of Beilstein for heterocyclic compounds was added to the lecture in spring 1989.

LOGISTICS

Coordination

The chemistry librarian coordinates and conducts all instruction. Close communication is maintained with faculty and students, which helps ensure that the logistics and lecture content are attuned to chemists' needs and schedules.

Classes

The two group lectures used for bibliographic and structure searching instruction rely on lectures, transparencies, and discussion. This format, begun in 1978, has been continued after evaluation of several options. Chemical databases are complicated and learning to search in an informed and efficient manner requires considerable time. However, chemistry seniors and researchers have extremely demanding and busy schedules, so three-hour or six-hour group sessions or more than two classes per topic are not acceptable. Therefore, immediate group practice on microcomputers that extends class time or frequency of classes would deter attendance. In addition, group practice requires that several additional librarians assist. In academia, this is difficult to arrange, because it is not common for several librarians in one school to have in-depth chemical expertise. This lack of sufficient expertise is a factor especially when working with researchers, because they bring their own laboratory-related questions. An option that was explored in 1989 is downloading a sample search for reuse with data projection equipment. This will recreate the search in a more realistic format than can transparencies. Using online demonstration during class, while providing realism and flexibility to answer "what if" questions, adds to class time without significant benefit. Such online demonstration requires a dataline, which can make locating a room extremely difficult given time constraints.

Other options under evaluation include use of STN Mentor[29] disks that incorporate some instruction in searching databases on the STN International system. This Mentor series employs computer aided instruction (CAI) techniques. There has been little additional effort to complete other CAI chemical searching programs, possibly due to the complexity of chemical databases.[30] Such options will be monitored for possible use.

Class size ranges from 10-23. Although smaller classes are preferred, all interested participants are accommodated in order to ensure that they receive training. With smaller classes, the second lecture can be scheduled sooner because fewer tutored sessions must be scheduled within the Academic Plan hours (Monday-Friday 5 p.m.-5 a.m. and Saturday until 1:00 p.m. Eastern time). Frequency of instruction must also consider the chemistry librarian's schedule. Two to three "courses" can be accommodated during an academic year.

Locating classrooms during times when attendees are available can be difficult. Seminar rooms are preferred. Few seminar rooms or classrooms include one or more datalines, so online demonstrations during the class would increase this difficulty.

Refreshments are served for undergraduates, who usually meet the first Saturday afternoon of the fall term. This is additional compensation for their willingness to give up prime enjoyment time. This amenity is not provided for researchers, who usually meet on weekday afternoons or evenings.

Tutored Practice

An online practice session is scheduled after each lecture for all attendees. This one-on-one tutored practice facilitates efficient learning and makes the best use of 3/4 - 1 1/2 hours of practice time. The discussion of the search process and results and sensitive encouragement by the instructor enormously aids understanding. This close interaction promotes rapport between the instructor and the "student." The length of practice sessions varies from 3/4 hours for the first bibliographic session to 1 1/2 hours for a structure search. Generally, the structure searches require longer appointments.

Initially, two chemistry seniors were selected as tutors to work along with the instructor for undergraduates' practice, but this required additional training time. When another librarian with chemical knowledge joined the staff, she replaced the two chemistry student tutors.

Because answers to the individualized researchers' questions cannot be prepared in advance, the chemistry librarian tutors all researcher practice sessions. This is time-consuming and it is difficult to schedule more than 2 or 3 per day due to the limited schedule of the CAS Academic Plan.

COSTS

Undergraduates

After the completion of the NSF grant, the Chemistry Department and Library share the cost of instructing chemistry seniors. The Library provides the manuals free of charge, other handouts, and the librarians' time. The Chemistry Department pays the cost of online searching.

Researchers

Researchers are charged $5 for each manual, which amounts to a registration fee. The cost of online practice is charged to research or departmental accounts. Costs involved in preparing the lectures and manuals are absorbed by the Library.

Post-Instruction Options

Many trained searchers prefer to use terminals located in their laboratories. However, terminals with datalines are available in the Library and are used occasionally. The imminent installation of STN Express on a public access microcomputer is expected to increase use of Library equipment. As SANDRA, the structure search guide to *Beilstein*, is publicized within the organic chemistry research groups, increased use of Library facilities is expected.

LIAISON ACTIVITIES

Undergraduates

Annual reports to the Chemistry Department Chairman, Library Representative, and Administrative Assistant, which review the computer search training and its cost, serve to keep the Department up-to-date. This written communication, along with informal and regular annual discussions with the Chairman, ensure the Department's continued financial support of the program.

Researchers

This training program enjoys the support of faculty in several University Departments. Each research group is encouraged to designate a person who coordinates its computer searching activities and who serves as a liaison with the librarian. Usually this is a graduate student, because faculty are generally too busy and post-doctoral fellows stay only a year or two. This liaison representative is most likely to bring questions about passwords, hardware, and software to the librarian, as well as search questions. The liaison generally does not receive documentation and newsletters directly but is dependent on receiving the material from his/her faculty advisor. A change in liaison representatives is sometimes known but in other cases learned when the next question arises.

SEARCH FREQUENCY

Undergraduates

Chemistry undergraduates occasionally search *Chemical Abstracts* online during their senior year. Some databases, such as the *Merck Index* and *Dictionary of Organic Compounds*, are easily accessed in print and not available on the vendor whose software they learned, so they are unlikely to be used. As other databases are added and as the *Beilstein* online file is extended back to volume 1 of the *Hauptwerk*, there will be greater use by undergraduates.

Researchers

Faculty who learn to search generally lack time needed to search and therefore rely on the librarian or a research group searcher to do their searches. In contrast, senior scientists, research associates, and other long-term staff generally continue to do their own searching. Post-doctoral fellows who stay one to two years are also likely to conduct their own searches. Graduate students, however, vary in their post-training search behavior. Sometimes the liaison representative becomes the group's searcher. Occasionally, several students in the group conduct searches because of their own interest. Some searches are referred to the librarian.

Search effectiveness varies by individual. There is a tendency to use a relatively small scope of commands and not to explore details because, while information gathering is a crucial part of conducting research efficiently, it is not the primary focus of the chemist. However, all who attend the training sessions learn about indexing and abstracting policies, contents of each record, and search strategies. This knowledge makes them more informed about when to request a search, what information to provide in stating the question, and what results to expect. As a result, they use computer searching more often.

STAYING CURRENT

Research groups vary in their handling of documentation. A minority of groups ensure that all searchers read newly-received updates. In most cases, the documentation is eventually or never transferred to the liaison by the faculty. Efforts to further disseminate the new information varies. As a result, many searchers do not update their searching knowledge or have their search skills reinforced.

A brief review (possibly two hours) of new search techniques and new databases is planned for 1989/90. This review would be open to all previous training attendees and would not involve online practice.

IMPACT OF PROGRAM

Researchers; Students

Attendees gain a greater awareness of and recognize the value of searching. Overall, participants have become more active users. Sometimes student usage has increased faculty interest. The additional information acquired through searches has facilitated research. Even when attendees do not conduct their own searches, they are more knowledgeable and prepare tentative search strategies.

Librarians

Teaching programs such as this one that includes developing and maintaining up-to-date manuals, planning and conducting lectures, and tutoring practice sessions requires an enormous amount of the trainer's time and energy. However, a program designed to meet the attendees' needs and with high quality interaction between the librarian and the attendees can accomplish a significant objective: to have the researchers and students recognize the librarian as an important information resource. The librarian is seen as working with the researches and teachers as a professional peer.

FUTURE

Graphics Input

The structure searching manual teaches text input of structures. In 1989/90 the instruction will expand to discuss structure input using graphics available in several software packages.

Full-Text Searching

Searching the full-text of journal and encyclopedia articles requires different search techniques. A one lecture unit will be planned to introduce researchers to these databases.

Reaction Searching

Reaction searching provides crucial information required for organic chemistry research. Several computerized databases currently permit structure searching of these databases, such as REACSS from Molecular Design Ltd. and CASREACT from Chemical Abstracts Service. A unit will be developed in 1989/90 to teach searching of these databases.

Numeric Searching

Numeric files for chemistry include special databases such as for *Beilstein*, *JANAF Thermochemical Tables* (U.S. National Institute for Standards and Technology), and the *NBS Tables of Chemical Thermodynamic Properties* (U.S. National Institute for Standards and Technology) and additional search capabilities within currently available databases such as INSPEC (*Science Abstracts*). These search features will be incorporated into the existing bibliographic instruction program as data relevant to the University community become available.

Bibliographic File Management

Use of bibliographic file management software will be reviewed in the bibliographic searching unit to a greater extent beginning in 1990.

Instruction Timing

Undergraduates

The use of SANDRA to locate Beilstein references was incorporated into the sophomore information instruction segment of organic laboratory in 1989. A review of other computerized instruction in 1990 will consider earlier inclusion in the instruction program.

Researchers

Training for researchers will be extended and modified to meet researchers' needs. Classes will continue to be scheduled throughout the academic year.

NOTES

1. Somerville, Arleen N.; Kende, Andrew S. Integrated Chemical Information Curriculum. National Science Foundation Grant No. 79-00761, April 1979-June 1982.

2. While questions targeted to the group and specific individuals are most effective, it is time-consuming to develop such lectures. Computer searching

modules that provide the lecture content are available without charge from the Division of Chemical Information (CINF), American Chemical Society. Modules available at this time include: Searching Chemical Abstracts (for both the DIALOG and STN International Systems); Searching chemical patents (for the DIALOG, ORBIT, or STN International Systems), and citation searching. Modules are available from this author.

3. Somerville, Arleen N. *Bibliographic searching of Chemical Abstracts (STN International Network): an introduction*. University of Rochester, Rochester, NY. October 1988 (Revised at least annually). Somerville, Arleen N. *Structure Searching in the Chemical Abstracts Service Registry File: An Overview*. University of Rochester, Rochester, NY. May 1989 (Revised annually).

4. Somerville, Arleen N. Computer searching by chemistry and pharmacology graduate students, post-doctoral fellows, and faculty at a research university; *Abstracts of Papers*, 188th American Chemical Society National Meeting, Philadelphia, August 26-31, 1984, CINF-04; Snow, Bonnie. Determining content and structure of online educational materials. In: *End user searching in the health sciences*. Edited by M.S. Wood; E. Brassil Horak; and B. Snow. New York: Haworth Press; 1986; p. 39-40.

5. Snow, Bonnie. Overview of End User Searching; Program sponsored by Association of College and Research Libraries (ACRL), Science and Technology Section; ACRL, Bibliographic Instruction Section, Reference and Adult Services Division, Machine-Assisted Reference Section. July 1, 1986, New York City.

6. DIALOG offers ONTAP training files for CA Search and Chemical Name databases, in addition to many related subjects such as biology, physics and medicine. Learning files are provided by STN International for CA File and The Registry File, as well as related subjects and databases such as the full-text of American Chemical Society journals.

7. Somerville, *Bibliographic Searching*, p. 2.
8. Somerville, *Bibliographic Searching*, p. 3.
9. Somerville, *Bibliographic Searching*, p. 4.
10. Somerville, *Bibliographic Searching*, p. 5.
11. Somerville, *Bibliographic Searching*, p. 6.
12. Somerville, *Bibliographic Searching*, p. 9.
13. Somerville, *Bibliographic Searching*, p. 11-13.
14. Somerville, *Bibliographic Searching*, p. 13.
15. Somerville, *Bibliographic Searching*, p. 13.
16. Somerville, *Bibliographic Searching*, p. 14.
17. Somerville, *Bibliographic Searching*, p. 20.
18. Somerville, *Bibliographic Searching*, p. 21.
19. Somerville, *Bibliographic Searching*, p. 22.

20. An introduction to computer searching: STN International Version. Prepared by the Education Committee, Division of Chemical Information, American Chemical Society, March 1986, p. 35-49.

21. Somerville, *Bibliographic Searching*, p. 1.
22. Somerville, *Structure Searching*, p. 2.

23. Somerville, *Bibliographic Searching*, p. 3.
24. Somerville, *Bibliographic Searching*, p. 5.
25. Somerville, *Structure Searching*, p. 9.
26. Somerville, *Structure Searching*, p. 9.
27. STN Express is front-end software that offers such features as automatic dialing and logon to STN, option to build text or structure queries offline, built-in designation of tautometers and normalized bonds, storage of queries, guided search option using menus, and predefined search strategies.
28. Structure and Reference Analyzer for Users of the Beilstein Handbook of Organic Chemistry. Version 2.0. 1987.
29. STN Mentor is a series of tutorials on floppy disks that help users learn about searching STN. Currently available disks include, for example, an STN Overview, an Introduction to CAS Online, author searching techniques, and searching biotechnology topics.
30. Ramsay, O. Bertrand. A Microcomputer Tutorial: introduction to online searching of chemical data bases. *Abstracts of Papers*, Third Chemical Congress of North America, Toronto, Canada, June 5-10, 1988, CINF-53.

SCI-TECH COLLECTIONS

Tony Stankus, Editor

The December 26, 1989, cover story of *Newsweek* was one example among many of the national attention being paid to the controversy over animal suffering in America's laboratories. Virtually every academic department of pharmacy, medicine, and psychology in the country, as well as a growing number of laboratories serving military, environmental, food, cosmetics, and industrial safety agencies has some experimental animals. Zoos and circuses are also under scrutiny. Many of these facilities are served by sci-tech-med librarians who are being pressed for information that will aid staff in complying with the law or in articulating institutional responses to aggrieved special interest groups. With this column, *Science & Technology Libraries* hopes to help those librarians. The authors present what we feel is a particularly earnest exploration of the documentation of some facets of primate management. The term "primates" include the apes, and apes have a need for special handling that respects their emotional as well as physical needs.

The Search for Psychological Well-Being in Captive Nonhuman Primates: Information Sources

Andrew J. Petto
Melinda A. Novak
Sydney Ann Fingold
Arlene C. Walsh

SUMMARY. Recent legislation and social pressures produced changes in the Animal Welfare Act, including a provision that requires environments that promote the "psychological well-being" of captive nonhuman primates. This paper focuses on the difficulties of both defining the concept of "the psychological well-being" of primates and identifying relevant documentation. An extensive literature review, on-line search strategy, and a listing of legal references, handbooks, guidelines, and update bulletins from agencies and associations are included, as are leads to audiovisual materials.

Andrew J. Petto holds a PhD in Physical Anthropology from the University of Massachusetts at Amherst. He chairs the Primatology Unit at Harvard Medical School, New England Regional Primate Research Center (NERPRC), where he also serves on the library committee. He has served as a member of the Animal Records Standardization Committee for the American Society of Primatologists, and the Animal Records Standardization working Group at the Institute for Laboratory Animal Resources. He was a coorganizer of the 1988 conference, The Psychological Well-Being of Captive Primates. Melinda A. Novak holds a PhD in Psychology from the University of Wisconsin at Madison. She chairs the Psychology Department at the University of Massachusetts at Amherst and is a visiting associate professor in Psychobiology at Harvard Medical School/NERPRC. She is a member of the Committee on Animal Research Ethics of the American Psychological Association, and the Advisory Panel to USDA on draft regulations for the psychological well-being of captive nonhuman primates. She was also a coorganizer of the 1988 conference, The Psychological Well-Being of Captive Primates.

© 1990 by The Haworth Press, Inc. All rights reserved.

INTRODUCTION

In an atmosphere of increasing concern and activism over animal welfare, the U.S. Congress approved revisions to the Animal Welfare Act (the Act) late in 1985.[1] This is the fourth revision to the Act since it was first passed in 1966. The new revision makes some specific recommendations about the care and use of captive animals, including a requirement that nonhuman primates be provided environments that enhance their psychological well-being.[2] The Department of Agriculture (USDA) — the federal agency charged with monitoring the implementation of the law — released a set of proposed regulations to achieve the goals specified in the Act in 1989.[3] The new regulations join the 37 existing legal and regulatory requirements for the use of animals in research and education.[4]

Understanding the new regulations and integrating them into existing animal husbandry programs is a complex task. All animal husbandry practices share the goal of improving the welfare of the

---

Sydney Ann Fingold holds a BS in Health Sciences Library Studies from the UWW Program at the University of Massachusetts at Amherst. She is currently the director of library services at the Harvard Medical School/NERPRC. She has held offices in the Massachusetts Health Sciences Libraries Network, Central Massachusetts Consortium of Health Related Libraries, and the North Atlantic Health Sciences Libraries (Regional Chapter of MLA). She was coordinator and chair of the ILL statistics Committee for Massachusetts Health Science Libraries. She is also a member of NENON and MLA. Arlene C. Walsh holds a BS in Psychology from the University of Massachusetts at Amherst. She is currently a research assistant in the Primate Ethology Subunit at Harvard Medical School/NERPRC.

This work was chiefly conducted at the New England Primate Research Center, a department of the Harvard Medical School, at 1 Pine Hill Drive, Southborough, MA 01772. There, Andrew J. Petto (PhD, U. Mass.) is Chair of Primatology, Sydney Ann Fingold (BS, U. Mass.) is Director of Library Services, and Arlene C. Walsh (BS, U. Mass.) is Research Assistant. Melinda A. Novak (PhD, Wisconsin) is Chair of Psychology at U. Mass., Amherst, MA 01003 and a Visiting Professor at the Primate Center. Contact Ms. Fingold for all library aspects of this paper. This work was supported in part by Division of Research Resources (NIH) Grant RR00168 to New England Regional Primate Research Center (NERPRC), and by funds provided by the American Psychological Association matching contributions from the University of Massachusetts at Amherst, Harvard Medical School (NERPRC), and the Tufts University School of Veterinary Medicine.

animals under our care. The literature provides many routes to achieving these goals among the many species, but perhaps none is as daunting as meeting the newest of the mandates—providing environments that promote the "psychological well-being" of captive nonhuman primates. We will use this part of the new regulations to illustrate strategies for retrieving important information about meeting this mandate and for gaining access to research in a variety of fields to produce an active program of animal care.

Because of the pressing practical need to understand the issues associated with "psychological well-being" and their complexity, we are using a new approach to reviewing the field. Our main purpose in this paper is to explore strategies for getting the most out of the available literature to help us understand the relationships of captive nonhuman primates to their environments and to other members of their group. We will also explore how these data help us to approach the issues raised by the "psychological well-being" regulations.

PSYCHOLOGICAL WELL-BEING IN CAPTIVE PRIMATES

Conspicuously absent from the new regulations is any working definition or specific statement as to what constitutes psychological well-being or what precisely we are meant to enhance in captive environments. The lack of definition reflects to a degree the diversity of the nonhuman primates whose well-being we are meant to enhance (there are over 200 distinct species). There are many differences among nonhuman primate species in the foods, friends, living accommodations, and "entertainment" that they prefer.[5-9] But mostly it reflects the injection of a nonscientific term—"psychological well-being"—into the understanding and interpretation of scientific data from animal behavior research. This makes understanding the literature and developing a search strategy very difficult.

Before the 1985 revision of the Act, researchers discussed environmental enrichment,[10-17] behavioral responses to environmental change,[18-23] or the frequency of expression of typical or atypical behaviors.[24-30] It was only after the inclusion of this phrase in the legislation that the phrase "psychological well-being" began to appear in the scientific literature. The first challenge for anyone trying to interpret this literature is to locate the large body of work containing important information about the interactions and associations among monkeys and between monkeys and their physical and nonphysical environments.

SEARCH STRATEGIES

Finding out about "psychological well-being" can be a daunting task. We used the resources of the Bibliographic Retrieval Service (BRS) to search for entries about "psychological well-being" in captive primates. The results are shown in Table 1. We also used the Primate Information Center (PIC) database maintained by the University of Washington in conjunction with the Washington Regional Primate Research Center (WaRPRC).

In all cases the search phrase "psychological well-being," even using several variants (wellbeing, well being, etc.), only retrieved six references that included this phrase in their titles.[31-36] The total number of "hits" on this search phrase was only 5 from 89 databases. Yet, a recent review by Woolverton et al.[37] contains 76 references, and our library maintains a partial database of relevant publications from 1988 that runs to 166 items.[38] The PIC database yielded 49 references from March and April, 1989 alone.

Table 1 shows the small number of references identified in the CROS utility maintained by BRS. CROS simultaneously searches a number of databases grouped by similarity of subject matter. Most databases yield a better result using "animal welfare" with "captivity" and "primates" as search terms (Strategy II), but these produced relatively few references. The most successful searches were based on phrases using "captivity" or "captive environments," "behavior," and "primates" (Strategy III).

One might be tempted to draw the conclusion from Table 1 that there is little scientific work on "psychological well-being" in nonhuman primates, but this would be incorrect. Strategy III shows that scientists are putting a great deal of effort into understanding the behavior of nonhuman primates in captivity and how that behavior is affected by different captive environments (see Table 2).

TABLE 1

SEARCH RESULTS BY BRS DATA BASE

Number of "Hits" by Number of Data Bases in Group

CROS DATA BASE GROUP	SEARCH STRATEGIES[1]		
	I	II	III
LIFE SCIENCES	0/15	2/15	9/15
MEDICINE/PHARM.	2/52	4/52	19/52
SOCIAL SCI./HUM.	3/25	2/25	6/25

[1]Search Strategies are as follows (see discussion in text).
I. Primate[s] and (psycholog[ical] well[-]being) and captiv[ity].
II. Primate[s] and welfare and captiv[ity].
III. Primate[s] and captiv[ity] and behavio[r].

The most productive databases for this strategy are BIOSIS (BIOL, BIOB), PsychINFO (PSYC), Social Sciences Citation Index (SSCI), and Zoological Record (ZREC). But it is important to remember that these numbers represent the sources that discuss *any* aspect of nonhuman primate behavior in captivity and may not be specific to the issue of "psychological well-being."

SUCCESSFUL SEARCHING

How can someone unfamiliar with the field of behavioral research among captive nonhuman primates produce a successful literature search? We think that there are two answers to that question. One involves choosing an appropriate database for the search, and the other involves careful consideration of the items being retrieved.

First, one should look to the databases that specialize in nonhuman primates, such as the PIC database (Appendix 5). It is certainly

TABLE 2
SEARCH RESULTS BY DATA BASE GROUP ON STRATEGY III

CROS DATA BASE GROUP

	LIFE SCIENCES	MEDICINE/PHARM.	SOCIAL SCI./HUM.
AIDD	1	1	*[1]
BIOB	44	44	*
BIOL	225	225	*
CABA	8	8	*
CAIN	4	*	*
CCML	*	29	*
CCON	14	14	14
DISS	16	16	16
EMEB	*	21	21
EMED	*	3	*
LLBA	*	*	1
MESH	*	23	*
MS82	*	15	*
MS76	*	8	*
MS71	*	1	*
NTIS	1	*	*
PSAL	*	8	8
PSYC	*	184	184
SSCI	*	*	120
ZREC	459	459	*

[1] '*' denotes data base not in group.

smaller than the BRS database, but it specializes in the literature about nonhuman primates and makes available new references monthly, including conference proceedings and published abstracts of presentations at scientific meetings. For example, abstracts of 45 papers and posters presented at a conference on psychological well-being in captive primates held in September, 1988, were indexed in the PIC database within two months after the conference was held and about a year before the publication of the proceedings by the American Psychological Association.[39]

Second, one should aim for quality, not quantity. There are two kinds of sources that help the reader to gain the most from the literature. The first reviews the major issues and developments in the field, such as that provided by Woolverton et al.[40] or Novak and Suomi.[41] These reviews report and discuss the relevant work of scientists concerned with issues in this area. The second provides a framework for approaching the problem by directing the discussion into a set of interrelated components, such as the papers collected in the proceedings of the 1988 conference in Boston.[42] This sort of resource looks to enhance our understanding of the field by directing the discussion toward salient, perhaps critical, issues that must be addressed in order to provide a coherent scientific basis for research and implementation of programs and policies.

Either of these sorts of resource is much more valuable to an unfamiliar searcher than a large number of references without any focus or direction. Some databases, such as Social Science Citation Index (SSCI), Magazine ASAP III (MSAP) or Psycholgical Abstracts (PSYC), will help the searcher determine which sort of reference s/he has found by providing abstracts, a list of references cited, or detailed summaries of the item cited.

For the remainder of this paper we will provide a brief example of the second sort of review. Although scientists may flinch at the term, "psychological well-being" is here to stay, and those who do research in this area must define the relevant issues and scientific foundations for the development of policies and programs. We contend that the issues raised by the need to promote and assess "psychological well-being" in captive nonhuman primates can be organized into four major areas—defining "psychological well-being," identifying and measuring it, interpreting and implementing programs and policies for its enhancement, and interacting with a concerned and active public to effect it.

DEFINING PSYCHOLOGICAL WELL-BEING

If there is agreement on any single issue in this field, it is that defining "psychological well-being" for captive nonhuman primates is a difficult and complex task (Novak and Suomi).[43] We *can* demonstrate that different conditions of captivity can produce changes in behavioral,[44-48] immunological,[49] neurochemical,[50,51] metabolic,[52,53] and developmental[54-56] variables. Yet none of these alone *is* "psychological well-being," just as none of these alone *is* physical well-being. Despite the many years of research that have demonstrated and confirmed these responses in captive nonhuman primates, there are two "traps" that await us in their application.

First, we can easily identify animals under stress, but not all stress is bad. It is a question of how the animal reacts to the stress that is the issue. We have identified both physiological and behavioral changes that indicate whether an individual is responding appropriately to stressors in the environment.[57-62] If we merely adjust the animal's environment so that the signs of distress disappear, we cannot claim that we have assured its well-being.[63] We may just have removed any interesting stimuli.

Second, we must avoid anthropomorphism. It is tempting to conclude that whatever humans like, monkeys like. Comparative studies of closely-related species at our Center and elsewhere[64-66] indicate that they behave significantly differently from *each other*. It is a mistake to overemphasize the obvious similarities to humans.

If we accept that "psychological well-being" is a complex phenomenon, then *many* observable features can be identified that relate to it—including behavior, health, reproduction, survival, etc. We think it is best to follow the suggestion of Novak and Suomi[67] who argue that the ability to adapt—to respond and adjust to changing situations—is the best general definition for psychological well-being. Under this plan, no single index would define "psychological well-being," but we would use a combination of observations from at least two of the variables that respond to environmental conditions.

IDENTIFYING AND MEASURING PSYCHOLOGICAL WELL-BEING

Many observable features have a relationship to "psychological well-being" through one of many interconnected "systems," such as the neuroendocrine[68] and reproductive systems.[69-71] When well-being is not present, then each of these systems shows some effect. However, the inverse may not be strictly true—that is, reproductive failures *could* be strictly due to physiological, genetic, or nutritional problems, even in psychologically "well" individuals.[72] The solution to this dilemma, of course, is to be able to rule out other potential causes by looking for a pattern to the problems.

The second issue is that the act of measurement can produce stress.[73,74] Although most of these procedures produce habituation over time, two problems remain. First, habituation to measurement procedures may give false assurance, since habituation decreases the behavioral and physiological responses to stimuli. Second, one must consider the practicality of the measurement. For example, behavioral profiles require little specialized equipment, a short training period, and minor disturbances of the animals. On the other hand, physiological measures based on blood or urine tests require more training, more equipment, and involve confining or immobilizing the animals temporarily to take the samples.

In the end, we probably should opt for behavioral measures, since behaviors integrate and express outwardly the inward condition of the animal vis-à-vis its social and physical environment. In addition, changes in behavior are easily recognized, and these monitoring procedures are practical to implement and noninvasive.

INTERPRETING AND IMPLEMENTING PROGRAMS AND POLICIES

The inclusion of "psychological well-being" in the amended Animal Welfare Act gives this mandate the force of law. The USDA regulations that follow this mandate also have the force of law. In a sense, there is little room for interpretation,[75] because the law and the USDA regulations require certain policies and procedures.[76-80]

This approach is different than that taken by the Public Health Service (PHS) in its guidelines for care and use of laboratory animals. The PHS guidlelines issued through the National Institutes of Health (NIH)[81] were developed by laboratory animal care specialists over several decades based on their knowledge and experience in the care of these animals.[82-84] For example, the behavior of nonhuman primates in laboratories has been studied for over 40 years. Animal care guidelines designed by these professionals allow a certain flexibilty of response while maintaining uniform standards. The changes and revisions to such professional guidelines are fairly quick and easy to make, especially in the case where they fail to meet the desired goals.

On the other hand, legislated procedures and policies are very difficult and take a long time to change, because of the nature of the regulatory process. The time, effort, and personnel necessary to change an ineffective or harmful regulation can result in more damage being done to the animals than the lack of any specific rules at all.

The best arrangement is a cooperative one between regulators and researchers. Regulators should be concerned with program and policy goals, and researchers should be developing scientifically based protocols for realizing these goals. (The USDA has implicitly recognized the value of the professional guidelines used by PHS by bringing many of its existing regulations into line with the PHS *Guide to the Care and Use of Laboratory Animals*.)[85] In addition, the research community ought to be involved in training the regulators and inspectors to keep them up to date in the field, making them more effective.

INTERACTING WITH A CONCERNED PUBLIC

Many people are concerned about the use of animals in research and their welfare.[86] Many do not know what research is going on, how it is carried out, or what it may mean to them. We are being deluged with information from nonscientists or "reformed" scientists about animal use and abuse. In some cases unrealistic images of the animals, their capabilities, and their "humanness" have been projected by the researchers themselves in an attempt to spark public interest in or improve public understanding of a species. In other cases, researchers have been reluctant to address public concerns about animal research directly or to be involved in outreach projects to their local communities and schools.[87,88]

There are two directions to take in addressing the relative lack of input that scientists have had to the public's perception of animal research. First, they can actively become involved to shape public's ideas about animals and animal research by teaching, communicating with the press, and speaking to various citizens' groups.[89-91]

Second, more scientists need to be made aware of the issues being raised by animal welfare advocates. Most professional research organizations and many journals have guidelines on the proper care and use of laboratory animals[92-97] (Appendix 3). Other organizations, such as the Scientists' Center for Animal Welfare (SCAW) are dedicated to understanding the necessary use of animals in research and maximizing the quality and quantity of data from each use in order to help reduce animal use in the future. In addition, much of the research with animals has either a stated goal or an expected outcome that the welfare of the study animals will be improved as a direct result of the research.[98] Such efforts should be made known to the public by the scientists involved in this work.

CONCLUSIONS

The welfare of laboratory animals is an area of many interrelated issues. It is possible to identify many biological and behavioral features that vary with the social and environmental conditions of captivity, but their relationship to any specific aspect of well-being (such as "psychological well-being") is complex.

This complexity makes fruitful searching a difficult task. We have proposed several solutions to this problem and provided an example of a limited, issue-directed search. In the absence of expertise in the specific area being searched, we recommend the use of specialized databases (Appendix 4), or those that provide more detailed information, such as abstracts or summaries, on the items that they include.

The current state of the field reflects the intrusion of a poorly-defined, nonscientific term, "psychological well-being" into the scientific literature. Trying to define it from the various studies of related phenomena is a little like trying to achieve the EPA estimates of gasoline mileage posted on new cars. We know that mileage is affected by type of fuel, tire pressure, road conditions, weather, and many other factors. None of these alone will assure reaching the EPA estimate, but paying attention to each will certainly improve the actual gas mileage we obtain. Indeed only some of these are within our control. It is only by examining how each of these elements relates to the others and to the goal (EPA estimate) that we can determine which changes produce the desired outcome.

The same is true of many animal welfare issues. Sometimes our expectations are disappointed or even frustrated, because the animals react to conditions in ways that we hadn't anticipated. Understanding these disappointments is the key to identifying and assuring "psychological well-being" in these captive animals. This may only be possible by a detailed search of the general animal behavior research, because large, complex puzzles are generally put together one small piece at a time.

REFERENCES CITED

1. Animal Welfare Act. *Federal Register* 50 CFR 17; 50 CFR 23. Washington, DC: Dec 31, 1985.
2. *Federal Register*. Op. Cit.
3. Animal Welfare—Standards. *Federal Register* 9 CFR 3. Washington, DC: Mar 15, 1989.
4. Knauff, D. Richard; Proposed animal welfare rules. *Lab Animal* 16:15-16, 1987.
5. Clarke, AS; Mason, WA; Moberg, GA. Interspecific contrasts in responses of macaques to transport cage training. *Laboratory Animal Science* 38:305-309, 1988.
6. Clarke, AS; Mason, WA; Moberg, GA. Differential behavioral and adrenocortical responses to stress among three macaque species. *American Journal of Primatology* 14:37-52, 1988.
7. Heymann, EW; Valdez, LA. Interspecific social grooming in a mixed group of tamarins, *Saguinus mystax* and *Saguinus fuscicollis* (Platyrrhini: Callitrichidae), in an outdoor enclosure. *Folia Primatologica* 50:221-225, 1988.
8. Small, Meredith F. Comparative social behavior of adult female rhesus macaques and bonnet macaques. *Zeitschrift fur Tierpsychologie* 59:1-6, 1982.
9. Clarke, AS; Mason, WA. Differences among three macaque species in

responsiveness to an observer. *International Journal of Primatology* 9(4):347-364, 1988.

10. Reinhardt, V; Houser, WD; Eisele, SG; Champoux, M. Social enrichment of the environment with infants for singly caged adult rhesus monkeys. *Zoo Biology* 6:365-371, 1987.

11. O'Neill, P. Developing effective social and environmental enrichment strategies for macaques in captive groups. *Lab Animal* 17:23-36, 1988.

12. Reinhardt, V; Houser, WD; Eisele, SG; Cowley, D; Vertein, R. Behavioral responses of unrelated rhesus monkey females paired for the purpose of environmental enrichment. *American Journal of Primatology* 14:135-140, 1988.

13. Fajzi, K; Reinhardt, V; Smith, MD. A review of environmental enrichment strategies for singly caged nonhuman primates. *Lab Animal* 18(2):23-35, 1989.

14. Crockett, CA; Bielitzki, J; Carey, A; Velez, A. Kong toys as enrichment devices for singly-caged macaques. *Laboratory Primate Newsletter* 28(2):21,1989.

15. Reinhardt, V; Cowley, D; Eisele, SG; Vertein, R; Houser, D. Preliminary comments on pairing unfamiliar adult female rhesus monkeys for the purposes of environmental enrichment. *Laboratory Primate Newsletter* 26:5-7, 1987.

16. Clough, G. Environmental effects on animals used in biomedical research. *Biological Reviews* 57:487-523, 1982.

17. Line, Scott. Environmental enrichment of laboratory primates. *Journal of the American Veterinary Medicine Association* 190:854-859, 1987.

18. Millar, SK; Evans, S; Chamove, AS. Older offspring contact novel objects soonest in Callitrichid families. *Biology of Behaviour* 13:82-96, 1988.

19. Bryant, CE; Rupniak, NM; Iversen, SD. Effects of different environmental enrichment devices on cage stereotypies and autoagression in captive cynomolgus monkeys. *Journal of Medical Primatology* 17:257-269, 1988.

20. Williams, LE; Abee, CR; Barnes, SR; Ricker, RB. Cage design and configuration for an aboreal species of primate. *Lab Animal Science* 38:289-291, 1988.

21. Rumbaugh, DM. Cage design attenuates display patterns of male chimpanzees. *Zoo Biology* 7:177-180, 1988.

22. Nash, LT; Chilton, S. Space or novelty?: effects of altered cage size on *Galago* behavior. *American Journal of Primatology* 10:37-49, 1986.

23. Macedonia, JM. Effects of housing differences upon activity budgets in captive sifakas (*Propithecus verreauxi*). *Zoo Biology* 6:55-67, 1987.

24. Boccia, ML. Preliminary report on the use of a natural foraging task to reduce agression and stereotypies in socially housed pigtail macaques. *Laboratory Primate Newsletter* 28:3-4, 1989.

25. Ross, RA; Giller, PS. Observations on the activity patterns and social interactions of a captive group of blackcapped or brown capuchin monkeys (*Cebus apella*). *Primates* 29:307-317, 1988.

26. Scucchi, S; Cordischi, C; Aureli, F; Cozzolino, R. The use of redirection in a captive group of Japanese monkeys. *Primates* 29:229-236, 1988.

27. Gust, DA. Uncertain availability of a preferred food affects choice in a captive group of chimpanzees (*Pan troglodytes*). *American Journal of Primatology* 17:165-171, 1989.

28. Johnston, PG; Rowell, TE. Social and environmental determinants of reproductive cycles in patas monkeys. *Internation Journal of Primatology* 8:223-243, 1987.

29. McGrew, WC. Parental division of infant caretaking varies with family composition in cotton-top tamarins. *Animal Behavior* 36:285-310, 1988.

30. Nieuwenhuijsen, K; de Waal, FBM. Effects of spatial crowding on social behavior in a chimpanzee colony. *Zoo Biology* 1:5-28, 1982.

31. Novak, MA; Suomi, SJ. Psychological well-being of primates in captivity. *American Psychologist* 43:765-773, 1988.

32. Novak, MA; Drewsen, KH. Enriching the lives of captive primates: issues and problems, in E Siegal (ed.) *Psychological Wellbeing of Captive Primates* NY: Noyes. (in press).

33. Coe, CL; Sheffler, J. Utility of immune measures for evaluating psychological well-being in nonhuman primates. *Zoo Biology* Suppl 1:89-99, 1989.

34. Novak, MA; Petto, AJ (eds). *The Psychological Well-Being of Captive Nonhuman Primates* Washington, DC: American Psychological Association, (in press).

35. Roberts, J. Environmental enrichment—psychological well being for people and primates. *American Journal of Primatology* 14(4):441-442 (abstract), 1988.

36. Wolfle, T; Whitney, R; Johnsen, D; Suomi, S; Stewart, W. The psychological well-being of primates—implementing new federal regulations. *American Journal of Primatology* 14(4):441-442 (abstract), 1988.

37. Woolverton, WL; Ator, NA; Beardsley, PM; Carroll, ME. Effects of environmental conditions on the psychological well-being of primates: A review of the literature. *Life Sciences* 44:901-917, 1989.

38. Fingold, SA (ed) *Environmental Enrichment and Psychological Well-Being of Nonhuman Primates Reference Database* Southborough, MA: New England Regional Primate Research Center; 1989.

39. Novak and Petto. Op. Cit.

40. Woolverton et al. Op. Cit.

41. Novak and Sumoi. Op. Cit.

42. Novak and Petto. Op. Cit.

43. Novak and Sumoi. Op. Cit.

44. Bryant et al. Op. Cit.

45. Chamove, AS; Bowman, RE. Rank, rhesus social behavior, and stress. *Folia Primatologica* 26:57-66, 1976.

46. Clarke et al. Op. Cit.

47. Rumbaugh. Op. Cit.

48. Pryce, CR. Individual and group effects on early caregiver-infant relationships in red-bellied tamarin monkeys. *Animal Behavior* 36:1455-1464, 1988.

49. Coe and Sheffler. Op. Cit.

50. Clarke et al. Op. Cit.

51. Ferraro, JS; Sulzman, FM. The effects of feedback lighting on the circadian drinking rhythm in the diurnal New World monkeys. *American Journal of Primatology* 15:143-155, 1988.

52. Clough. Op. Cit.

53. Ferraro and Sulzman. Op. Cit.

54. Wilson, ME; Gordon, TP; Rudman, CG; Tanner, JM. Effects of a natural versus artificial environment on the tempo of maturation in female rhesus monkeys. *Endocrinology* 123:2653-2661, 1988.

55. Chapais and Larose. Op. Cit.

56. Altmann, J; Altmann, S; Hausfater, G. Physical maturation and age estimates of yeallow baboons, *Papio cynocephalus*, in Amboseli National Park, Kenya. *American Journal of Primatology* 1:389-399, 1981.

57. Clarke et al. Op. Cit.

58. Chamove and Bowman. Op. Cit.

59. Barnard, N; Hou, S. Inherent stress—The tough life in lab routine. *Lab Animal* 17(6):21-27, 1988.

60. Moberg, GP. Problems in defining stress and distress in animals. *Journal of the American Veterinary Medicine Association* 191:1207-1211, 1987.

61. Suomi, SJ; Kraemer, GW; Baysinger, CM; Delizio, RD. Inherited and experiential factors associated with individual differences in anxious behavior displayed by rhesus monkeys, in Klein, F; Rabkin, J (eds.) *Anxiety: New Research and Changing Concepts* New York: Raven Press. pp. 179-200, 1981.

62. Spinelli, JS; Markowitz, H. Prevention of cage-associated distress. *Lab Animal* :19-23.

63. Peterson, EA. Noise and laboratory animals. *Laboratory Animal Science* 30(2):422-438, 1980.

64. Clarke and Mason. Op. Cit.

65. Small. Op. Cit.

66. Heyman and Valdez. Op. Cit.

67. Novak and Suomi. Op. Cit.

68. Coe and Sheffler. Op. Cit.

69. Johnson, LD; Petto, AJ; Sehgal, PK. Survival and reproduction as measures of psychological well-being in cotton-top tamarins (*Saguinus oedipus*), in Novak, MA; Petto, AJ (eds). *The Psychological Well-Being of Captive Nonhuman Primates* Washington, DC: American Psychological Association, (in press).

70. Scullion, FT. Husbandry, breeding, and maintenance of a viable population of cotton top tamarins (*S. oedipus*). *Animal Technology* 38:167-174, 1987.

71. Beck, BB; Power, ML. Correlates of sexual and maternal competence in captive gorillas. *Zoo Biology* 7:339-350, 1988.

72. Seier, JV. Breeding vervet monkeys in a closed environment. *Journal of Medical Primatology* 15:339-349, 1986.

73. Barnard and Hou. Op. Cit.

74. Hoeprich, PD; Wolfe, BM; Jerome, C; Olson, DA; Huston, AC. Long-

term venous access in rhesus monkeys. *Antimicrobial Agents and Chemotherapy* 21(6):976-978, 1982.

75. Hunt, RD. The necessity for interpretation of standards designed to promote psychological well-being of nonhuman primates, in: Novak, MA; Petto, AJ (eds). *The Psychological Well-Being of Captive Nonhuman Primates* Washington, DC: American Psychological Association, (in press).

76. Meyers, N. Government regulation of nonhuman primate facilities. *Journal of Medical Primatology* 12:169-183, 1983.

77. Stewart, WC. Legal standards for human care: The Animal Welfare Act. *Lab Animal* 13(6):33-41, 1984.

78. Knauff. Op. Cit.

79. Black, HS; Doepel, FM. Legislation, policy, attitudes impacting ARF management. *Lab Animal* 14:40-43, 1985.

80. Wolfle, TL. Nonhuman primates in research: Trends in conservation, importation, production, and use in the United States. *Lab Animal* 12(3):19-27, 1983.

81. Public Health Service, *Guide for the Care and Use of Laboratory Animals*, NIH Publication No. 86-23. Washington, DC: Department of Health and Human Services; 1985.

82. Wolfle. Op. Cit.

83. Wolfle, TL. Psychological well-being: The billion dollar solution, in Novak, MA; Petto, AJ (eds). *The Psychological Well-Being of Captive Nonhuman Primates* Washington, DC: American Psychological Association, (in press).

84. Hunt. Op. Cit.

85. Public Health Service. Op. Cit.

86. Weber, H. Democratic expression of public opinion on animal experimentation. *Journal of Medical Primatology* 15:379-389, 1986.

87. King, FA. Public information: The foundation for continuing support of primate research, in: Novak, MA; Petto, AJ (eds). *The Psychological Well-Being of Captive Nonhuman Primates* Washington, DC: American Psychological Association, (in press).

88. Bennett, BT. Translating research into workable regulations, in: Novak, MA; Petto, AJ (eds). *The Psychological Well-Being of Captive Nonhuman Primates* Washington, DC: American Psychological Association, (in press).

89. Dodds, WJ. Public perception concerning research with captive primates and other animals, in: Novak, MA; Petto, AJ (eds). *The Psychological Well-Being of Captive Nonhuman Primates* Washington, DC: American Psychological Association, (in press).

90. King. Op. Cit.

91. Friedman, SM; Dunwoody, S; Rogers, CL (eds). *Scientists and Journalists* New York: MacMillan; 1986.

92. Ellery, AW. Guidelines for the specification of animals and husbandry methods when reporting the results of animal experiments. Working Committee

for the Biological Characterization of Laboratory Animals/GV-SOLAS. *Lab Animals* 19:106-108, 1985.

93. American Psychological Association. Guidelines for ethical conduct in the care and use of animals. Washington, DC: APA, 1985.

94. American Behavior Society. Guidelines for the use of animals in research. *Animal Behavior* 43:315-318, 1986.

95. Boakes, RA. Guidelines for the use of animals in research. *Quarterly Journal of Experimental Psychology* 38B:111-116, 1986.

96. American Society of Mammologists. Acceptable field methods in mammalogy: Preliminary guidelines approved by the American Society of Mammalogists. *Journal of Mammalogy* 68(4):Suppl, 1987.

97. Committee on the Care and Conservation of Chimpanzees. Recommendations to USDA on improving psychological well-being for captive chimpanzees. *Journal of Medical Primatology* 17:71-76, 1988.

98. Loew, FM. Animals as beneficiaries of biomedical research originally intended for humans. *ILAR News* 30(4):13-20.

APPENDIX 1

LEGISLATION

FEDERAL REGISTER: Volume 54/No. 49/Wednesday, March 15, 1989
9 CFR Part 3 [Docket No. 87-004]
ANIMAL WELFARE – STANDARDS
Proposed Rules pp. 10897-10954

FEDERAL REGISTER: December 31, 1985 (Revised)
50 CFR 17
50 CFR 23 There is one law (the Animal Welfare Act of 1966, as amended in 1970, 1976, and 1985) plus regulations developed by one federal agency (the National Institutes of Health), that cover most of the animals used for research and testing in the United States.

CONGRESSIONAL RECORD: Volume 131/No. 175/Dec. 17, 1985
Congressional Record – House
H 12335

Text of "The Improved Standards for Laboratory Animals Act"

FISH & WILDLIFE FACTS
U.S. DEPARTMENT OF THE INTERIOR
Non-Human Primates   FWS-F-035   March 1985

Order from: Federal Wildlife Permit Office
Fish and Wildlife Service
U.S. Dept. of the Interior
Washington, D.C. 20240
(703) 358-2104

HEALTH RESEARCH EXTENSION ACT OF 1985
Public Law 99-158, November 20, 1985
"Animals in Research"

Order from: The Office of Protection from Research Risks
Public Health Service
NIH
Building 31 – Room 4B09
Bethesda, MD 20892
(301) 496-7041

APPENDIX 2

ASSOCIATIONS: POLICIES AND GUIDELINES

PUBLIC HEALTH SERVICE POLICY ON HUMANE CARE AND USE OF LABORATORY ANIMALS

Order from: Office for Protection for Research Risks (OPRR)
Policy and Assurance Staff
National Institutes of Health
Building 31 – Room 4B09
Bethesda, MD 20892
(301) 496-7041

NIH GUIDE FOR GRANTS AND CONTRACTS
Special Edition: LABORATORY ANIMAL WELFARE
Volume 14, No. 8, June 25, 1985

Order from: Division of Research Resources
NIH
Building 31 – Room 5B59
Bethesda, MD 20205
(301) 496-4000

AAALAC ACTIVITIES REPORT AND DIRECTORY OF MEMBERS OF THE COUNCIL ON ACCREDITATION AND ACCREDITED LABORATORY ANIMAL FACILITIES
American Association for the Accreditation
of Laboratory Animal Care
9650 Rockville Pike
Bethesda, MD 20814
(301) 530-7000

AALAS BULLETIN
American Association for Laboratory Animal Science
70 Timber Creek Drive
Suite 5
Cordova, TN 38018
(901) 754-8620

ACCEPTABLE FIELD METHODS IN MAMMALOGY: PRELIMINARY GUIDELINES APPROVED BY THE AMERICAN SOCIETY OF MAMMALOGISTS
Supplement to *Journal of Mammalogy* 68: November 1987 (No. 4)

American Society of Mammalogists
Department of Zoology
Brigham Young University
Provo, UT 84602
(801) 378-2006

ASSOCIATIONS: ANIMAL RIGHTS/WELFARE

DIRECTORY OF ANIMAL RIGHTS/WELFARE ORGANIZATIONS
National Association for Biomedical Research (NABR)
818 Connecticut Avenue, NW
Washington, DC 20006
(202) 857-0540

ASSOCIATIONS: TRAINING

LATA NEWSLETTER
Laboratory Animal Training Association
12616 Waterman Drive
Raleigh, NC 27614
(919) 846-5969

MANUAL FOR LABORATORY ANIMAL TECHNICIANS
American Association for Laboratory Animal Science (AALAS)
70 Timber Creek Drive
Cordova, TN 38018
(901) 754-8620

APPENDIX 3

HANDBOOKS AND GUIDES

GUIDE FOR THE CARE AND USE OF LABORATORY ANIMALS
U.S. Department of Health and Human Services
Public Health Service, National Institutes of Health
NIH Publication No. 86-23 (Rev. 1985)

For sale by: Superintendent of Documents, U.S. Government Printing Office, Washington, DC 20402

USE OF LABORATORY ANIMALS IN BIOMEDICAL AND BEHAVIORAL RESEARCH
Committee on the Use of Laboratory Animals in Biomedical and Behavioral Research. The Commission on Life Sciences. National Research Council. Institute of Medicine. 1988

For sale by: National Academy Press, Div. of National Academy of Sciences, 2101 Constitution Ave., NW, Washington, DC 20418

THE BIOMEDICAL INVESTIGATOR'S HANDBOOK FOR RESEARCHERS USING ANIMAL MODELS
Foundation for Biomedical Research 1987

For sale by: Foundation for Biomedical Research, 818 Connecticut Ave., NW, Washington, DC 20006

THE UFAW HANDBOOK ON THE CARE & MANAGEMENT OF LABORATORY ANIMALS
Trevor Poole, editor. Sixth Edition 1987

For sale by: Longman Scientific & Technial, Longman Group UK Limited, Longman House, Burnt Mill, Harlow, Essex CM20 2JE, UK

GUIDE TO THE CARE AND USE OF EXPERIMENTAL ANIMALS
Canadian Council on Animal Care. Volume 1 1980

For sale by: Canadian Council on Animal Care, 1105-151 Slater Street, Ottawa, Ontario K1P 5H3, Canada

EFFECTIVE ANIMAL CARE AND USE COMMITTEES
Edited by F. Barbara Orlans, Richard C. Simmonds, W. Jean Dodds.
Laboratory Animal Science (Special Issue) January 1987 or
Scientist Center for Animal Welfare, 4805 St. Elmo Avenue, Bethesda, MD 20814

LABORATORY ANIMALS: AN INTRODUCTION FOR NEW EXPERIMENTERS
Tuffery, A.A. (Editor)
John Wiley & Sons., New York 1987

LABORATORY ANIMAL HOUSING
Institute of Laboratory Animal Resources, Division of Biological Sciences, Assoc. of Life Sciences. Proceedings of a Symposium 1978

For sale by: National Academy of Sciences, 2101 Constitution Ave., NW, Washington, DC 20418.

HEALTH BENEFITS OF ANIMAL RESEARCH
Gay, William I. (Editor)

For sale by: Foundation for Biomedical Research, 818 Connecticut Ave., NW, Washington, DC 20006.

APPENDIX 4
ADDITIONAL RESOURCES

Bibliographies

National Institutes of Health
Specialized Bibliography Series

LABORATORY ANIMAL WELFARE
Order: SBS No. 1986-1, SBS No. 1987-1, SBS No. 1988-1
Cost: Free (Send mailing label)
From: National Library of Medicine
  Public Services Division
  Bethesda, MD 20894

National Agricultural Library
Quick Bibliography Series

WELFARE OF EXPERIMENTAL ANIMALS
January 1979-September 1988
Issued JANUARY 1989 (331 Citations)

Order: NAL-BIBL QB89-18
   Updates QB88-17
Cost: Free (Send mailing label)

ANIMAL WELFARE LEGISLATION AND REGULATION
January 1979-November 1988
Issued FEBRUARY 1989 (301 Citations)

Order: NAL-BIBL QB89-23
   Updates QB88-40
Cost: Free (Send mailing label)

Both bibliographies available
From: U.S. Department of Agriculture
   National Agricultural Library
   Beltsville, MD 20705

Primate Information Center
University of Washington
Topical Bibliography Series

Order: 86-019 CAGES, CORRALS & CONSEQUENCES: HOUSING MONKEYS IN THE LAB COLONY 1976-1986 ($6.50)
Order: 87-011 ENVIRONMENTAL ENRICHMENT FOR CAPTIVE NONHUMAN PRIMATES 1972-1987 ($4.50)
Order: 86-015 LEGAL REQUIREMENTS, IMPORT REGULATIONS & THE WELFARE ISSUE: NONHUMAN PRIMATES IN LAB COLONIES 1981-1986 ($5.50)

Also available: Monthly and Retrospective CUSTOM Bibliographies
   (Send for Information and Fee Schedule)
From: Primate Information Center
   Regional Primate Research Center (SJ-50)
   University of Washington
   Seattle, WA 98195
   Phone: (206) 543-437 FAX: (206) 545-0305

Scientists Center for Animal Welfare
USDA National Agricultural Library
Laboratory Animal Welfare Bibliography

Order: LABORATORY ANIMAL WELFARE BIBLIOGRAPHY December 1988 (and 1989 supplement) ($15.00)
From: Scientists Center for Animal Welfare
4805 St. Elmo Avenue
Bethesda, MD 20814

Journals

American Journal of Primatology
Animal Behavior
Folia Primatologica
International Journal of Primatology
Journal of Medical Primatology
Lab Animal
Lab Animal Science
Zoo Biology

Newsletters

ILAR NEWS (QUARTERLY)
Institute of Laboratory Animal Resources
2101 Constitution Avenue, NW
Washington, DC 20077-5576

LABORATORY PRIMATE NEWSLETTER (Quarterly)
Primate Behavior Laboratory
Psychology Department
Brown University
Providence, RI 02912

SCIENTISTS CENTER FOR ANIMAL WELFARE NEWSLETTER (Quarterly)
Scientists Center for Animal Welfare
4805 St. Elmo Avenue
Bethesda, MD 20814

THE ANIMAL WELFARE INSTITUTE QUARTERLY
Animal Welfare Institute
P.O. Box 3650
Washington, DC 20007

LABORATORY ANIMAL MANAGEMENT REVIEW (Quarterly)
Laboratory Animal Management Assoc.
P.O. Box 1744
Bethesda, MD 20902

ANIMAL KEEPERS' FORUM (Monthly)
American Association Zoo Keepers, Inc.
635 Gage Blvd.
Topeka, KS 66606

AAZPA NEWSLETTER (Monthly)
American Association Zoological Parks & Acquariums
Oglebay Park
Wheeling, WV 26003-1698

Audiovisuals

Environmental Enrichment for Individually Caged Rhesus Monkeys at the WRPRC

78 slides illustrate methods developed to enrich the environment of caged Rhesus monkeys used in research protocols.

Facilitated Socialization of Previously Singly Caged Adult Rhesus Monkeys

VHS Videotape 1/2" (20 Minutes) In Color—focuses on methods for housing Rhesus monkeys in pairs within the research setting.

BOTH AVAILABLE ON LOAN FROM: Audiovisual Services
Wisconsin Regional Primate Research Center
1223 Capitol Court
Madison, WI 53715-1299
(608) 263-2513

Audio Cassette Tapes

Science and Animals: Addressing Contemporary Issues 1988

    1. Recognizing the "Well-Being" of Laboratory Primates
       (45 Minutes) Melinda Novak/Stephen Suomi $12.00
    2. What is "Suffering"?
       (45 Minutes) Eric Cassell $12.00
    3. Can Animal Use Be Ethically Justified
       (90 Minutes) J. Wesley Robb $15.00
       —plus 12 other tapes (Entire Set $175.00)

Well-being of Laboratory Animals 1987

    1. Responsibilities of Investigators and Institutions
       W. Jean Dodds (SCAW) $12.00
    2. The History of Laboratory Animal Legislation
       Christine Stevens (Animal Welfare Inst.) $12.00
    3. Primates in the Wild and in Captivity: Environments,
       Behavior, and Welfare. Jeanne Altmann $12.00
       —plus 4 other tapes (Entire Set $70.00)

BOTH SETS OF AUDIO CASSETTE TAPES AVAILABLE FROM:

    Scientists Center for Animal Welfare (SCAW)
    4805 St. Elmo Avenue
    Bethesda, MD 20814

An Audiovisual Bibliography

"Audio-visuals in the Collections of the National Agricultural Library relating to ANIMAL WELFARE" June 1988

BIBLIOGRAPHY AVAILABLE FROM:
    National Agricultural Library
    Animal Welfare Information Center
    Public Services Division
    Beltsville, MD 20705
    (301) 344-3755

APPENDIX 5
MISCELLANEOUS INFORMATION SOURCES

Animal Welfare Information Center

The Animal Welfare Information Center (AWIC) of the National Agricultural Library (NAL) offers an expanding collection of books, journals, newsletters, proceedings, reports, news articles, slides, films, and video recordings of interest to those interested in the welfare of laboratory animals. The AWIC was created through the Improved Standards for Laboratory Animals Act of 1985 (The Dole-Brown Amendment to the Animal Welfare Act).

NAL and AWIC holdings are open during regular business hours. Information requests may be placed by mail, telephone, or in person. The collection may also be accessed by computer. User fees are charged for work requiring over an hour of staff time or $25 in computer time. For further information, contact AWIC, Room 301, National Agricultural Library, 10301 Baltimore Blvd., Beltsville, MD 20705, (301) 344-3755.

Primate Information Center

The Primate Information Center (PIC) was established in 1963 to provide information, based on the scientific literature, to scientists throughout the World and is the only literature search service providing direct access to bibliographic information on any species of nonhuman primate.

All searching is done on a unique database, developed and maintained by the PIC staff. Staff members review articles on all phases of primate research and describe their contents in terms of the species of primate studied and the type of research involved. There is a vocabulary of approximately 5000 terms. This computer generated database is not publicly available. Requests for service may be placed by letter or telephone. Contact the Primate Information Center, Regional Primate Research Center (SJ-50), University of Washington, Seattle, WA 98195, (206) 543-4376.

CAB International

CAB INTERNATIONAL (CABI), formerly the Commonwealth Agricultural Bureaux, is a cooperative not-for-profit organization owned, administered, and financed by member governments. The chief function of the Information Services is to provide ready access to published information on research in agriculture and allied disciplines. The CAB ABSTRACTS

Database is publicly accessible online from major internationa online vendors and from CABI. For further information, write CAB International, Farnham House, Farnham Royal, Slough SL2 3BN, UK.

National Library of Medicine

The National Library of Medicine offers the MEDLINE database (the online version of INDEX MEDICUS) through their MEDLARS system. A service desk is staffed at NLM to answer questions about the online system. The desk is staffed between 8:30 A.M. and 5:00 P.M. Monday through Friday. Phone: (800) 638-8480 or (301) 496-6193. Write: National Library of Medicine, 8600 Rockville Pike, Bethesda, MD 20209.

Biosciences Information Services (BIOSIS)

BIOSIS PREVIEWS is produced by the world's largest life sciences information service, from information published in *Biological Abstracts* and *Biological Abstracts/RRM*. BIOSIS PREVIEWS is available through BRS, Dialog, STN, CAN/OLE, DATASTAR, DIMDI, ESA/IRS, and CISTI. For further information contact: Biosciences Information Service, 2100 Arch Street, Philadelphia, PA 19103, (800) 523-4806 or (215) 587-4800.

NEW REFERENCE WORKS IN SCIENCE AND TECHNOLOGY

Arleen N. Somerville, Editor

Reviewers for this volume are: Laura Delaney (LD), New York Public Library; Collette Holmes (CH), Rensselaer Polytech Institute, Troy, NY: Isabel Kaplan (IK), University of Rochester; Kathleen Kehoe (KMK), Columbia University; Donna Lee (DL), University of Vermont; Ellis Mount (EM), Columbia University; Arleen Somerville (ANS), University of Rochester.

EARTH SCIENCES

Dictionary of the environment. 3rd ed. By Michael Allaby. New York: New York University Press; 1989. 423p. $70.00. ISBN 0-8147-0591-X.

    This concise dictionary defines a wide variety of environmental terms and concepts. In addition to covering standard vocabulary in the field, it outlines the policies and/or purposes of various governmental and non-governmental environmental agencies as well as international environmental institutions. This edition includes an expanded number of entries in the field of nuclear power and a separate table listing major environmental disasters of recent years. Definitions are clear and succinct and many cross references are provided. Suitable for environmental science collections of all levels. (LD)

The field guide to geology. By David Lambert and the Diagram Group. New York: Facts on File; 1988. 256p. $22.95. ISBN 0-8160-1697-6.

The earth's evolution from the creation of the solar system to the present day provides the focus for this basic field guide. Intended for amateur geologists of all ages, this heavily illustrated work contains over 500 maps, charts, and diagrams. A myriad of topics are explored including continental evolution, volcanic landforms, glaciers and ice sheets, and geological prospecting. Appendices list the achievements of famous geologists and various geological displays around the world. A subject index and a brief bibliography are provided. Recommended for public libraries and personal collections. (LD)

Meteorology source book. Edited by Sybil P. Parker. New York: McGraw-Hill; 1988. 304p. $40.00. ISBN 0-07-045511-2. (The McGraw-Hill Science Reference Series)

This handy reference guide brings together all the meteorological information scattered throughout the *McGraw-Hill Encyclopedia of Science & Technology* (6th edition, 1987). A range of basic terms and concepts are defined from paleoclimatology to meteorological instrumentation and weather forecasting. In addition, a separate weather section describes such natural phenomena as cyclones, monsoons, hurricanes, and waterspouts. Numerous illustrations, charts, and graphs enhance the text and a subject index and brief chapter bibliographies are provided. A good, basic reference source for public and academic libraries. (LD)

Practical handbook of environmental control. Edited by Conrad P. Straub. Boca Raton, FL: CRC Press; 1989. 537p. $45.00. ISBN 0-8493-3707-0.

Based on information published in the 5-volume *CRC Handbook of Environmental Control*, this book is intended for professionals and students in the fields of public health, environmental science, and municipal and industrial waste. Information is presented in tabular form and is broken down into 5 main sections: air, water sources and quality, wastewater, solid wastes, and institutional considerations. The tables cover a multitude of subjects from the properties of some typical aerosols to the composition of municipal refuse. In addition, most tables cite the source of their data, an extremely useful feature. Numerous references and a substantial subject index are provided. Recommended for environmental science and public health collections of all levels. (LD)

ENGINEERING AND TECHNOLOGY

Communications satellite handbook. By Walter L. Morgan and Gary D. Gordon. New York: Wiley; 1989. 900p. $69.95. ISBN 0-471-31603-2.

This book is aimed toward advanced students, technicians, engineers, professors, planners, regulators, and others in the electrical engineering profession. This book is divided into five major parts: teletraffic, communications satellite systems, multiple access techniques, space craft technology, and satellite orbits; each section includes a detailed table of contents. Each section is self-contained, so that a reader can go directly to the topic of his or her interest. Lists of symbols, constants, and acronyms are also included, as well as extensive lists of references at the end of each chapter. (CH)

Computer-integrated manufacturing handbook. By V. Daniel Hunt. New York: Chapman and Hall; 1989. 322p. $57.50. ISBN 0-412-01651-6.

This title does not fall strictly into the area of mechanical engineering. However, manufacturing is an area of interest to most disciplines in engineering and especially mechanical engineering, so as a manufacturing engineering handbook, this work will be of interest to mechanical engineers. Written as an easy-to-read, basic introduction, it provides a good overview to manufacturing engineering for mechanical engineers. The main body of the book is organized simply into four sections that cover fundamentals, applications, technology assessment, and competitiveness. Appendices serve as ready reference tools giving lists of CAD/CAM organizations and manufacturers, acronyms, and abbreviations, as well as an extensive bibliography. (CH)

The dictionary of SDI. By Harry Waldman. Wilmington, DE: Scholarly Resources, Inc.; 1988. 182p. $35.00 (Hard cover); $19.95 (Paperback). ISBN 0-8420-2281-3 (Hard cover); ISBN 0-8420-2295-3 (Paperback).

This *Dictionary* defines nearly 800 terms in the areas of ballistic missile defense, arms control, research and development, counter-moves to defense, Soviet capabilities, the roles of U.S. allies, personalities in the field, and SDI software and hardware. (ANS)

Essential circuits reference guide. By John Markus and Charles Weston. New York: McGraw-Hill; 1988. 531p. $59.50. ISBN 0-07-040462-3.

During his 27-year career with McGraw-Hill, the late John Markus authored 15 books for the publishing company. The material in this book brings together circuits published from three of these books: *Modern Electric Circuits Reference Manual*, *Electronic Circuits Manual*, and *Guidebook of Electronic Circuits*. While this book only includes a small part of what was included in Markus' three earlier books, the authors state that it presents the classics in electronic circuits. This volume incorporates errata for the earlier publications. In most cases the circuit elements listed are still available from the original manufacturer.

For each circuit the following information is included: values of significant components, identifying titles, concise descriptions, performance data and suggestions for applications. In addition to this, references are included to the original source for the circuits. Mailing addresses for these sources are also included so that readers may write for back issues or articles. Arranged into 62 sections covering various types of circuits such as automotive, music, telephone or infrared circuits, the authors feel that most users will be able to use the book's table of contents to locate specific circuits. They also have included a detailed subject index to aid access. Although a collection of previously published information, libraries with limited budgets or space will be interested in this title. (CH)

Handbook of reliability engineering and management. Rev. ed. Edited by W. Grant Iverson and Clyde V. Coombs, Jr. New York: McGraw-Hill; 1988. Mixed pagination. $59.50. ISBN 0-07-032039-X.

Reliability is an extremely important aspect to all areas of engineering, and this reliability handbook covers the area while paying special attention to electrical engineering. Originally published in 1966 under the title: *Reliability Handbook*, this book is written for managers as well as practicing engineers. The book is divided into three sections: introduction to reliability; management of reliability; and engineering for reliability. Within these sections, chapters are authored by experts from the field who are for the most part professionals working in the electrical engineering industry. Its appendices consist of tables and charts. (CH)

Handbook on anaerobic fermentations. Edited by Larry E. Erickson and Daniel Yee-Chak Fung. (Bioprocess technology, vol. 3). New York: Marcel Dekker; 1988. 850p. $149.75. ISBN 0-8247-7974-6.

This volume in the series Bioprocess technology focuses on the biotechnology and biochemical engineering of anaerobic fermentation. Its intended audience is biochemical and environmental engineers, and applied microbiologists and biochemists. In 23 chapters the book's contributors cover the microbiology of anaerobic species; biochemistry, kinetics, and transport in anaerobic fermentation; bioenergetics and yield of these processes; measurement and data analysis; the nature, engineering and modelling of mixed culture interactions; and reactor design and application of anaerobic processes. Each chapter includes a bibliography. The volume is indexed. (IK)

How to get it—a guide to defense-related information resources. Compiled by Gretchen A. Schlag. Cameron Station, Alexandria, VA: Defense Technical Information Center: 1989. 626p. AD-A201600. Available from: National Technical Information Service, Springfield, VA 22161. $55.95.

Updating the previous edition issued in 1982, this document provides an index to the hundreds of prefixes or identifiers used in conjunction with reports and similar publications issued by the many units within the Department of Defense. For example it lists NAVDOCK P-127 as being issued by the Naval Facilities Engineering Command and as being superseded by NAVFAC-127. There are many cross references plus a 13-page bibliography of documents having to do with the preparation and control of military publications. (EM)

LANs explained: a guide to local area networks. By W. Scott Currie. New York: Halsted Press; 1988. 208p. $39.95. ISBN 0-470-21063-x.

The chief audience for this publication is managers and technical staff who may purchase LANs. Since LANs is undoubtedly one of the most important technologies of the 1980s, others looking for an introduction to this subject will find this book of interest as well. Although the author contends he has written his book as a cross between a "full-blooded technical book and an idiot's guide," he has actually done an excellent job of providing an overview to LANs. The book includes an introductory section that gives definitions and discusses the current state of the art for LANs, as well as a technology section that presents applications for LANs and introduces generic topology and access techniques. A separate section examines the major LANs that have been the focus of standardization, as well as the most popular LANs. A fourth section discusses protocols and standards, and a fifth section outlines the future of LANs. Careful attention is given to American organization such as the IEEE (Institute of Electrical and Electronics Engineers) who are involved in this field. So, although this is essentially a British publication, U.S. readers will find it useful. (CH)

Optics in education; a guide to optics programs in North America. 1987-88 edition. Society of Photo-Optical Instrumentation Engineers: 1988. 46p. Available without charge from: Rich Donnelly, SPIE, P.O. Box 10, Bellingham, WA 98227. no ISBN

Published annually, this is the primary listing of optics programs in North America. Each entry provides the following information: director of program; graduate and undergraduate program contacts; address and phone number of program and contacts; degrees granted; number of undergraduate and graduate students; academic and research specialties; research facilities; industry/university cooperative programs; tuition; admission policies and requirements; admission deadlines; scholarships and grants; and faculty names with specializations. An indispensable guide for comprehensive descriptions of academic optics programs. (ANS)

Roark's formulas for stress and strain. 6th ed. By Warren C. Young. New York: McGraw-Hill; 1989. 763p. $56.25. ISBN 0-07-072541-1.

The format of this new edition follows that of the 5th edition which relied on the ever-increasing user-friendly software available for problem solving. And, like its predecessor, this edition addresses the need for more precise treatment of engineering problems. The main body of Roark's book is divided into three sections: definitions; facts, principles, and methods; and formulas and examples. Chapters are accompanied by extensive bibliographies, and an author index is included at the end of the text to provide access to these articles. An appendix lists factors of stress concentration. A detailed table of contents, along with a subject index provides excellent subject access. Roark's handbook is a classic in the field and should be part of most engineering collections. (CH)

HEALTH SCIENCES

Bowes and Church's food values of portions commonly used. 15th ed. Revised by Jean A. T. Pennington. Philadelphia: Lippincott; 1989. 328p. $18.50. ISBN 0-397-54727-7.

Both generic and name brand foods are listed. In addition to providing values for calories, proteins, cholesterol, fats, and vitamins, this book contains supplementary tables for amino acids, biotin, caffeine, salicylates, and other food components. The appendix also includes a bibliography of additional sources for food composition data. The index, like the entire publication, is very thorough. Possibly the most complete book of this kind. (DL)

Directory of national self-help/mutual aid resources. Chicago: AHA; 1987. 269p. $27.25. ISBN 0-87258-465-8.

In order to gather data for this directory, the Illinois Self-Help Center sent questionnaires to more than 900 organizations concerned with over 250 health issues, from abortion to Turner Syndrome. International, national, or regional organizations with a self-help focus are described. For topics where no larger organization exists, the directory lists addresses and phone numbers for state and local organizations. Toll-free hotlines are also included. (DL)

Drug companies & products world guide. By Marshall Sittig and Janne S. Kowalski. Kingston, NJ: Sittig and Noyes; 1988. 596p. $120. ISBN not given.

Data extracted from the Pharmaceutical Manufacturing Encyclopedia, by the same publisher, have been rearranged and updated to form this publication. The Encyclopedia outlines raw materials consumed, reaction conditions, and product separation techniques for each drug. This Guide lists only the company name, address, phone number, and a sampling of products for each company. Over 2,000 US and 2,000 foreign companies are arranged alphabetically by company name. The Guide would be far more valuable with indexes for generic and trade names for drug products, and an index by country and state. (DL)

Duncan's dictionary for nurses. 2nd ed. By Helen A. Duncan. New York: Springer Publishing; 1989. 802p. $18.95. ISBN 0-8261-6200-2.

This paperback dictionary briefly defines almost 20,000 terms found in nursing and clinical medicine literature. Many terms are specific to nursing, such as: aftercare, Nurses House Inc., and TABS. Twelve appendices include Abbreviations Used in Prescription Writing, Nursing and Nursing-Related Organizations, Nursing Journals, and Nursing Diagnoses Approved by the North American Nursing Diagnosis Association. Nurses will also want access to a standard medical dictionary since some medical terms cannot be found in this dictionary. (DL)

Health, United States, 1988. Washington, DC: GPO; 1989. 208p. $16. ISBN not given.

Appearing annually, this publication includes 29 charts and 125 statistical tables describing health status, health resources, and cost of health care in the United States. Each year the focus of the publication changes. This edition highlights smoking, heart disease, stroke, lung cancer, breast cancer, suicide, mesothelioma, coal workers' pneumoconiosis, acute leukemia, and bladder cancer. Many of the tables rely on unpublished data from the National Center for Health Statistics; other tables provide references to published statistical sources, allowing for further research. (DL)

The medical book of lists: a primer of differential diagnosis in internal medicine. 2nd ed. By Norton J. Greenberger, Kent Berquist and others. Chicago: Year Book Medical Publishers; 1987. 293p. $15. ISBN 0-8151-3944-6.

Compiled by three chief residents and one professor of medicine, this book presents over 230 lists designed to aid residents in arriving at a diagnosis. Lists range from a classification of dementia, to 19 causes of polyuria, to a list of criteria for a diagnosis of irritable bowel syndrome. This book is especially valuable in reference collections because many of the lists cite other books and journal articles. (DL)

Resources for comparative biomedical research: a directory of the DRR Animal Resources Program. Prepared by Research Resources Information Center. Bethesda: NIH; 1988. 74p. Free. ISBN not given.

The Animal Resources Program of the NIH Division of Research Resources has published this directory to publicize the resources available through their three subprograms: the Regional Primate Research Centers Program; the Laboratory Animal Sciences Program; and the Biological Models and Materials Resources Program. The directory lists the centers involved in each program, the resources they can provide (e.g., diagnostic services), and an outline of their current research. (DL)

Specialty profiles. 1988 ed. By Mary Ann Eiler and Thomas J. Pasko. Chicago: AMA; 1988. 906p. $70. ISBN 0-89970-339-9.

Entries for 20 specialties describe the historical development of each specialty and provide a wide range of statistics, including the number of specialists by school, year of graduation, sex, and location. Medical students deciding on a specialty, as well as public policy researchers and administrators concerned with physician supply, will find this book useful. (DL)

Third opinion: an international directory to alternative therapy centers for the treatment and prevention of cancer. By John M. Fink. New York: Avery Publishing; 1988. 268p. $14.95. ISBN 0-89529-382-X.

This guide to alternative and adjunctive therapy programs concentrates on nutritional, metabolic, "immune-enhancing," and behavioral-psychological modalities. Entries for treatment centers, educational centers, support groups, and information services provide one-page synopses of the services offered, costs, addresses, and phone numbers. Written by a man who spent two years pursuing therapies for his daughter, who ultimately died of cancer, the chapter on Guidelines for Choosing a Therapy is both helpful and realistic. (DL)

LIFE SCIENCES

Artifacts in biological electron microscopy. Edited by Richard F.E. Crang and Karen L. Klomparens. New York: Plenum Press; 1988. 233p. $45.00. ISBN 0-306-42863-6.

Biologists use electron microscopes to examine the cellular, subcellular and macromolecular details of plant and animal tissue. Preparing the specimens involves different ways of slicing, fixing, staining, and embedding them. This process frequently results in the production of artifacts which may resemble cell structures. There have been many instances where researchers have assumed that an artifact is a part of the cell structure or vice versa. "One classic example of the initial failure to distinguish between artifact and native structure is the Golgi Apparatus, which was originally thought to be an artifact."

The book includes many electron micrographs illustrating the most commonly encountered artifacts. In addition, it is a laboratory manual covering all the current preparation methods used in transmission and scanning electron microscopy. It is the only current volume on this topic and it will be very useful to libraries serving biological scientists. (KMK)

Atlantic Fishes of Canada. Can. Bull. Fish Aquat. Sci. vol. 219. By W.B. Scott and M.G. Scott. Toronto, The University of Toronto Press; 1988. 731p. ISSN 0706-6503. $110.00

This is a completely rewritten edition of Leim and Scott's 1966 "Fishes of the Atlantic Coast of Canada." (*Can. Bull. Fish Aquat. Sci. vol. 155.*) The volume includes many newly identified species as well as additional data on species covered by the previous edition. Each family has a brief entry with general information on the family's characteristics. Following this are the species entries which include: common and scientific names of the species, a black and white sketch of the fish, the person and date of first observation, and the following data: habitat, reproduction, growth, food, predation and competition, parasites and disease, distribution, relation to man, and systematic notes.

The volume includes a 55-page bibliography including biological and fishing industry literature on the different species. It also has a glossary, a checklist of species, an index of common and scientific names, a metric conversion table and color photographs of some common fishes.

This comprehensive work is an excellent reference tool for Life Sciences collections. (KMK)

European handbook of plant diseases. Edited by I.M. Smith et al. Oxford, New York: Blackwell Scientific Publications; 1988. 583p. $125.00. ISBN 0-632-01222-6.

"The aim of the European handbook of plant diseases is to provide a comprehensive treatment of the diseases of cultivated plants and major forest and amenity trees in Europe." The authors have chosen to emphasize diseases which affect crops which are economically important such as grape vines. Garden plants which are commercially grown are included, but wild plants have been omitted.

The book is organized by pathogen, not by disease. One or more chapters is devoted to diseases caused by viruses, rickettsia, bacteria, oomycetes, ascomycetes, chytridiomycetes, and basidiomycetes. The pathogens are presented in alphabetical order within each chapter. Each entry includes a brief description of the pathogenic organism, host plants and diseases, identification and diagnosis, epidemiology, geographic distribution, economic impact and methods of control. There are two indexes: a host index and a pathogen index. This volume is recommended for large agricultural collections. (KMK)

PHYSICAL SCIENCES

Data book on the viscosity of liquids. By D.S. Viswanath and G. Natarajan. New York: Hemisphere Publishing Corp.; 1989. 990p. $275.00. ISBN 0-89116-778-1.

Viscosity data are provided for over 900 compounds, including organic compounds, inorganic liquids, liquid metals, lubricants, plasticizers, and foods like soybean oil. Viscosity values are provided at different temperatures. Also listed for each compound are at least one primary journal reference and usually the Chemical Abstracts Service Registry Number. A common name index is provided. A major source for viscosity data. (ANS)

Encyclopedia of physical sciences and engineering information sources. Edited by Steven Wasserman, Martin A. Smith and Susan Mottu. Detroit: Gale Research; 1989. 736p. $140.00. ISBN 0-8103-2498-9.

Lists important sources of information on 425 subjects in the fields of science and engineering. For example, under the subject of Air Pollution the editors have selected nine abstract services, a yearbook, two professional associations, two bibliographies, six directories, two encyclopedias, two monographs, two handbooks, five online databases, one newsletter, five periodicals and four research institutes. Thus any single major source such as a major database might be listed in scores of subjects throughout the book. All items were found to be in print at the time of publication. Each entry includes the name, address and telephone number of the publisher or source plus the price of the item. There are numerous cross references in the index and throughout the subject listings. An interesting approach, which would undoubtedly provide librarians and researchers quick assistance in many instances. (EM)

Handbook of data on organic compounds. 2nd ed. Edited by Robert C. Weast and Jeanette G. Grasselli. Boca Raton, Fla.: CRC Press; 1989. 9 vols. ISBN 0-8493-0420-2 (set).

This greatly expanded 2nd edition provides physical properties and spectral data for 26,000 of the most common organic compounds. Entries list molecular weight, boiling point, melting point, density, refractive index, specific rotation, color, and solubility. Spectral data given includes infrared, Raman, ultraviolet, nuclear magnetic resonance, and mass spectroscopy. Each entry also includes the Chemical Abstracts Service (CAS) Registry Number, reference to the Beilstein *Handbuch der Organischen Chemie*, CAS index name, synonyms, structure, and line and molecular formulas. Entries are alphabetical by CAS index name, but indexes by synonyms (up to 100,000 synonyms) and molecular formula aid location of entries. Other indexes provided are by melting point, boiling point, molecular weight, and spectral data for each type of spectra. Derivatives not available in similar handbooks can be found here. Although the cost is high, the 9-volume set is valuable for undergraduate and research chemistry collections. Annual supplements are planned. (ANS)

Handbook of polycyclic hydrocarbons. By Jerry Ray Dias. Amsterdam: Elsevier; 1988. Physical Sciences Data, vol. 30B. $155.25. ISBN 0-444-43007-5 (vol. 30B).

This second volume of a two-volume set focuses on polycyclic conjugated hydrocarbons, while the first volume dealt with polycyclic aromatic hydrocarbons. As with its companion volume, a discussion of nomenclature and molecular graphs precede the listing of known chemical and physical properties, including spectra. Journal references are usually provided. (ANS)

Name reactions and reagents in organic synthesis. By Bradford P. Mundy and Michael G. Ellerd. New York: John Wiley & Sons; 1988. 546p. $39.95. ISBN 0-471-83626-5.

Information about more than 120 common named reactions and over 145 of the most commonly used reagents in organic synthesis is provided in this indispensable volume. For each reaction, the following information is presented: general reaction scheme, reaction scheme showing mechanism, selected reaction examples, and journal references for the examples. Information provided for reagents include structure, physical properties, major uses, preparation, precautions, representative examples of uses, and references for the examples and to Fieser's *Reagents for Organic Synthesis* series. An essential title for all libraries serving organic synthesis students, faculty, and other researchers. (ANS)

Optics source book. Sybil P. Parker, Editor-in-Chief. New York: McGraw-Hill Book Co.; 1988. 399p. $48.00. ISBN 0-07-045506-6.

Extracted from the *McGraw-Hill Encyclopedia of Science and Technology*, this book groups information related to optics. Chapters cover such topics as geometrical optics, imaging systems, wave optics, lasers, interaction of light with matter and with energy, light detection and processing, measurement of light, and human perception of light. References are provided at the end of each section. This book serves as a portable reference book on the topic of optics. (ANS)

Solid-state physics source book. Sybil P. Parker, Editor-in-Chief. New York: McGraw-Hill Book Co.; 1988. 381p. $48.00. ISBN 0-07-045503-1.

Extracted from the *McGraw-Hill Encyclopedia of Science and Technology*, this book brings together material on the physical properties of solids, such as electrical, dielectric, elastic, and thermal properties, and their relation to fundamental physical laws. These topics are of special interest to research areas such as superconductivity. Serves as a portable reference book. (ANS)

Spectroscopy source book. Sybil P. Parker, Editor-in-Chief. New York: McGraw-Hill Book Co.; 1988. 288p. $43.00. ISBN 0-07-045505-8.

Extracted from the *McGraw-Hill Encyclopedia of Science and Technology*, this book brings together information about spectroscopy from the physics perspective. Chapters deal with atomic and molecular spectroscopy, nuclear spectroscopy, microwave and radio frequency spectroscopy, mass spectroscopy, and instrumentation and techniques. References are provided within each chapter. Serves as a portable reference book. (ANS)

SCIENCE, GENERAL

Better scientific and technical writing. By Morris I. Bolsky. Englewood Cliffs, NJ: Prentice Hall; 1988. 195p. $14.95. ISBN 0-13-074253-8.

Written in a terse, lucid style, this book is a practical guide to writing scientific and technical documents. It focuses on the principles of good writing, addressing such topics as accuracy, clarity, and readability. Problematic elements of grammar and punctuation are reviewed and various aspects of production are examined including printing and distribution. A subject index and references are provided. Recommended for sci/tech libraries of all levels and for personal collections. (LD)

European research centres: a directory of scientific, technological, agricultural, and medical laboratories. 7th ed. Compiled by Longman editorial team. Harlow, Essex, UK: Longman; 1988. (Dist. by Gale) 2 vols. 2093p. $455.00 per set. ISBN 0-582-00601-5.

The latest edition of this established reference source profiles 17,000 laboratories and departmental research centers in 31 European countries (Note: The Soviet Union is not covered.) Arranged alphabetically by country, this guide covers industrial research laboratories in public and private corporations, government laboratories, research-funding organizations, and university departments and research institutes. Entries include such information as: organization title, address, telephone number, telex address, facsimile number, director's name, number of graduate research staff, annual expenditures, and a list of organizational activities and publications. In addition, major laboratories are now highlighted with a star before the title. Entries may be accessed through the subject index or the establishment name index. An excellent reference source for any sci/tech research collection. (LD)

Handbook of effective technical communications. By Tyler G. Hicks and Carl M. Valorie. New York: McGraw-Hill; 1989. mixed pagination. $49.50. ISBN 0-07-028781-3.

Written for scientists, technical writers, and engineers, this practical handbook supplies tips and suggestions on how to write more effectively. Various forms of technical communication are covered including reports, articles, specifications, proposals, technical papers, books, catalogs, instruction manuals, sales brochures, and letters. Guidelines on conducting research and outlining are provided, as well as a review chapter on grammar and word usage. Suitable for sci/tech collections of all levels and for personal use. (LD)

Handbook of research laboratory management. By Virginia P. White. Philadelphia: ISI Press; 1988. 240p. $49.95. ISBN 0-89495-065-7.

This detailed handbook serves as a guide to the administration of research laboratories. The author has held a number of high level administrative posts including Assistant Director at Oak Ridge National Laboratory's Biology Division and Director of Operations at the Salk Institute. Among the topics considered are recruiting a research team, obtaining and administering grants, laboratory safety, buildings and equipment, and financial resources. One chapter discusses the library within the research laboratory. A subject index is provided as well as a limited number of chapter references. Institutional executives involved in research and laboratory directors are the intended audience. (LD)

Information resources for engineers and scientists—workshop notes. 5th ed. By Charlie Maiorana. Washington: INFO/tek; 1989. (42 chapters numbered separately.) $95.00.

Material for this book grew out of lecture notes and class materials for a workshop on information resources for engineers in the defense industry. It presents an overview of sources of technical information that are readily accessible to the informed researcher and information provider. Quite thorough in its coverage of types of sources (technical reports, patents, standards, journal articles, translations, dissertations, etc., etc.), it serves not as a comprehensive bibliography, but rather claims as its purpose to raise the "information consciousness" of its readers, give them a "working knowledge of major information resources," and an understanding of databases for information retrieval. All of which will make them better able to formulate requests for information clearly and with realistic expectations. The book is doubly useful to librarians—for its material on sources, but also as a model for teaching and learning about information. Despite its emphasis on defense-related works, it will be enlightening to anyone seeking to research topics in science and technology. (IK)

Isaac Asimov's book of science and nature quotations. Edited by Isaac Asimov and Jason A. Shulman. New York: Weidenfeld and Nicolson; 1988. 360p. $19.95. ISBN 1-555-84111-2.

More than 2,000 science and nature quotations are covered in this useful and entertaining guide. It includes both obscure and well-known quotes in 86 different categories ranging from aeronautics to zoology. Within each subject area, quotations are arranged chronologically by the date of the quotation itself or, if unavailable, by the birth date of the speaker. Entries also include a brief description of the speaker (e.g., Orville Wright, American Inventor/Aviator, 1871-1948). A useful index of speaker names provides an additional point of access. Recommended for sci/tech collections of all levels. (LD)

SCI-TECH ONLINE

Ellen Nagle, Editor

TENTH NATIONAL ONLINE MEETING

The 1989 National Online Meeting, held in May in New York City, offered 85 technical papers, exhibits, product reviews, and several satellite events. More than 95 product reviews and 110 exhibits provided over 1600 conference attenders with information on the spectrum of electronic databases and services. For the second year, the meeting included a separate CD-ROM Gallery with 26 exhibits and demonstrations of optical products.

In recognition of this tenth anniversary meeting, the plenary session featured a presentation by Program Chairman Martha Williams entitled "Highlights of the Past Ten Years in the Online Database Industry." A panel, comprising a "who's who" of information industry pioneers, reacted to Williams' presentation. Panelists included Everett Brenner, Jan Egeland, Donald Hawkins, and Roger Summit.

Technical papers centered around several major themes. Topics covered such diverse areas as: artificial intelligence and information retrieval; hypertext and hypermedia, image databases; the information services environment; quality control; legal constraints to generating, communicating and using electronic data; generating full text databases; specialized databases; and CD-ROM. New this year was "a conference within a conference." Integrated Online Library Systems '89 (IOLS) had its own set of plenary sessions, technical papers, exhibits and product reviews. The theme of the conference was "Mainframes, Minis, and Micros: Maximizing Resources Through Appropriate Choices."

DATABASE NEWS

Enhanced Biocommerce Abstracts and Directory

Biocommerce Abstracts has been expanded to include an international directory of biotechnology organizations. The new name, *Biocommerce Abstracts and Directory*, reflects the enhanced coverage of the database. Approximately 1,000 directory records were added initially. That number is expected to increase significantly. Most of their listings describe United States and European biotechnology companies, but coverage also includes some universities, nonprofit organizations, research institutes, and firms that supply the industry.

Each directory record contains the full name of the company; its address, telephone, telex, and telefacsimile numbers; a descriptive summary covering history, investors, product lines, research, numbers of staff, and names and titles of key executives. Controlled index terms describe major business areas. The price for searching *Biocommerce Abstracts and Directory* is now $1.75 per minute. Records printed on or offline cost $1.50 to $2 per record, depending on format selected.

PDQ Patient Information File (PDQI) on BRS

BRS is offering *PDQI*, a source of easy to comprehend information for the cancer patient. Developed and produced by the National Cancer Institute, the database is one of several PDO files offered by BRS. The files are designed to provide information about the dynamic state of cancer treatment, standards of care and therapeutic options.

Searchers can turn to *PDQI* for patient education summaries on 80 cancer types that describe prognosis, treatment options and expectations. As an instructional tool written in simple, easy to understand language, the database helps the cancer information patient know what to expect. It also aids doctor-patient communication. The prognostic and treatment information available in the *PDQ* databases was developed and refined with the assistance of more than 400 cancer specialists who served as reviewers and medical consultants. An Editorial Board of 72 prominent oncologists maintains the currency and accuracy of the information and updates the contents of the summaries based on new data.

Micro Software Directory

The *Micro Software Directory* (*SOFT*) is now searchable on DIALOG as File 237. Produced by Online, Inc. of Weston, Connecticut, the database lists business and professional microcomputer software products currently available in the United States. It provides directory, product, and bibliographic information on leading software packages.

The *SOFT* database is highly selective, according to DIALOG. It lists programs rated at least "good" by the technical press, all packages from major producers (even if negatively reviewed), and packages unique to specific business segments. In addition, major emphasis is given to library and medical software. Listings are provided free to software publishers selected for inclusion. A large percentage of the current records contain representative reviews; different points of view are reflected by multiple reviews. There is no print counterpart to the file.

SOFT records are written and edited by information professionals who scan major technical journals and product literature including brochures, factsheets, and press releases. Each record provides directory information, as well as hardware and other technical specifications required to run the software. Concise product descriptions are written by Online, Inc. staff. Citations to reviews and brief evaluative abstracts are included. Controlled vocabulary is used to index the "application" field.

Micro Software Directory contains approximately 5,000 records. It is updated monthly with 100 new or updated records. The price for searching File 237 is $1.10 per minute. The cost of printing online or offline citations is $.60 per record.

CRISP Subfile in Federal Research in Progress

Federal Research in Progress contains records describing the ongoing research projects funded by a number of United States government agencies. The database is compiled by the National Technical Information Service (NTIS). They receive the database records from the various agencies that are represented and merge them into a single database. DIALOG makes the database available as File 266 (unabridged and available only in the United States), and File 265 (does not contain Department of Energy or NASA records; available worldwide). The *CRISP (Computer Retrieval of Information on Scientific Projects)* subfile represents the largest portion (60-70%) of *Federal Research in Progress* records.

CRISP is developed by the National Institutes of Health (NIH) and contains reports of research funded by various agencies of the U.S. Public Health Service. These agencies include NIH; the Alcohol, Drug Abuse and Mental Health Administration (ADAMHA); the National Institute of Occupational Safety and Health; the Food and Drug Administration; the Bureau of Health Professions; and the National Center for Health Services Research. *CRISP* represents the single largest source of information on ongoing developments in biomedical research in the United States.

The subfile contains not only records of extramural projects (research grants and contracts), but also records of NIH and ADAMHA intramural research (projects carried out in the laboratories of the various institutes of these two agencies). *CRISP* provides insight into new and emerging research areas, often well before any mention of them is made at conferences or in the published literature. *CRISP* records reflect research in its earliest stages, important to researchers preparing grant applications or to those who are interested in certain kinds of instrumentation, techniques, or procedures. The *CRISP* subfile is divided into two segments representing the two most recent fiscal years.

PUBLICATIONS AND SEARCH AIDS

Zoological Record Serial Sources

BIOSIS has announced the publication of a new reference source *Zoological Record Serial Sources*. It is an annual publication that contains complete listings for all serials scanned for *Zoological Record* online. In addition to the more than 5,000 serials listed, the publication includes separate lists of new, ceased, and changes titles. Included in this reference source are full title, abbreviated title, CODEN, publication frequency, publisher number, and pertinent history notes. Also included is a complete list of publishers, their addresses, and a list of the titles they publish. *Zoological Record Serial Sources* is priced at $35 per copy. To order, contact: BIOSIS, Marketing Section, 2100 Arch Street, Philadelphia, PA 19103-1399. Telephone: (800)523-4806; (215)587-4800.

1989 MeSH Chemical Tool

Medical Subject Headings—Supplementary Chemical Records, 1989 may be ordered from the National Technical Information Service (NTIS). The *Chemical Tool* contains records of approximately 21,000 chemicals that since 1970 have been mentioned in a significant way in journals indexed in *MEDLINE*. Records include information on the name of the substance; Chemical Abstracts Service Registry number or Enzyme Commission number; related registry numbers; synonyms; pharmacological action; indexing information; and miscellaneous notes. Prices for the hardcopy version are $30 in the United States and Canada and $60 elsewhere. The microfiche version cost $14.50 in the U.S. and Canada and $29 elsewhere. Shipping and handling charges are $3 (U.S. and Canada) and $4 elsewhere. The document should be ordered as PB89-113054/GBB. Order from: National Technical Information Service, 5285 Port Royal Road, Springfield, VA 22161. For telephone orders with deposit account or credit card, call (703)487-4650.

CRISP Search Aids

A number of publications are available to help in searching the *CRISP* subfile of *Federal Research in Progress*. The *CRISP* Thesaurus can be ordered from NTIS (address same as above). The order number for the current edition is PB88-189477. The price for the hardcopy version is $56.95 for U.S. orders; $113.90 for non-U.S. orders. Microfiche copies are $14.50 and $29 respectively. Two additional publications are available free of charge: *NIH Manual Issuance 4101 (Activity Codes, Organizational Codes, and Def-*

initions used in Extramural Programs) and *What is the CRISP System?* Both of these publications can be requested by sending a self-addressed mailing label to the research Documentation Section, Information Systems Branch, Division of Research Grants, National Institutes of Health, 5333 Westbard Avenue, Room 148, Bethesda, MD 20892.

SCI-TECH IN REVIEW

Karla Pearce, Editor

FAX IT TO ME

Brown, Steven Allen. Telefacsimile in libraries: new deal in the 1980's. *Library Trends*. 37(3): 343-56; 1989 Winter.

Three great improvements in telefacsimile transmission: greater compatibility among machines, greater speed of transmission, and lower cost—have caused libraries to re-consider this technology. This literature review covers recent developments in telefacsimile technology and describes costs and benefits experienced by libraries and users. However, the technology is still not perfect—there are still problems with paper jams, document legibility can be a problem and costs are still not inconsiderable. However, the options fax offers to encourage library networking may offer one answer to the problem of making better use of our collections. (KJP)

SYSTEMS ANALYSIS FOR YOUR NEXT PROJECT

Main, Linda. CPM and PERT in library management. *Special Libraries*. 39-44; 1989 Winter.

CPM (Critical Path Method) and PERT (Program Evaluation Review Techniques) are used widely in business and government to manage complex projects. However, because they chart critical pathways that specify steps that are followed in success view stages of a project, they can be used to plan and manage library projects as well. Using network diagrams to illustrate the practical limitations of a job and its sequential relationships, the author shows PERT and CPM techniques and how they might be used in libraries. However, such projects need no longer be done manually; computer programs such as Milestone, Timeline, Quickplan and Superproject can do it for you. The more complicated your next project is, the more you may need the help of one of these project managers. (KJP)

MEMEX — HYPERTEXT?

Nyce, James M.; Kahn, Paul. Innovation, pragmatism, and technological continuity: Vannevar Bush's Memex. *Journal of the American Society for Information Science*. 40(3): 214-220; 1989 May.

For everyone who has heard, read or thought about Vannevar Bush's famous memex, as described in his 1945 essay in the *Atlantic Monthly*, "As We May Think," this article gives us an interesting historical perspective. He also quotes from Bush's subsequent writings on information retrieval and gauges how far we have progressed towards achieving that dream. In later writings, (1955) Bush pointed out that although "we are making great strides in developing the means for the transmission of ideas from one to another . . . we are making little progress . . . in finding in the record the information we need." Many might agree that, in 1989, we are far from solving this problem. Enter hypertext. Although you may not agree with the "hype" that has followed this more associative mode of information retrieval, it is clearly closer to Bush's evolving concept of an analytical machine for retrieving information. However, the author admits, "with all the technological progress made during the 1980's, a hypertext system that approaches memex still strains the limits of the available technology." Perhaps the extensive storage offered by CD-ROM will make a difference? (KJP)

COLLECTING SOFTWARE

Pascoff, Beth M. Microcomputer software in library collections. *Library Trends*. 37(3): 320-15; 1989 Winter.

Issues relating to selection, purchase, classification, storage, circulation and copyright of software in libraries are discussed. Although libraries often claim that format should not be a strong factor in materials' selection, monetary, technological and legal problems have discouraged us from adding software to our collections. The author lists nine criteria for software selection, from documentation to user friendliness, lists publications that review new software, notes cataloging problems, e.g., the rules for cataloging machine readable data files were published in 1978, and discusses potential (and real) problems of damage and copyright violations. At this time just 38% of all ARL libraries circulate computer software. An extensive bibliography on the subject makes this a valuable source for anyone contemplating making computer programs available to their users. (KJP)

80 WAYS TO CHANGE YOUR LIBRARY

Rapp, Brigid; Marzetti, Loretta. Blueprint for the vital library. *Information Management Review*. 4(3): 49-54; 1989.

Librarians must focus their efforts so that they conform to the expressed and implied needs of the organization they serve. The EPA's Information Services Branch of the Office of Information Resources and Management manages the headquarters library and coordinates the network of 28 EPA libraries. A case study of some improvements in this organization's activities reveals how they have identified needs, designed a user friendly collection, developed a database for access to their materials on hazardous wastes, and provided for continuing assessment of their efforts. To help you achieve similar success, the authors posit many practical suggestions for an action plan you can use. (KJP)

CONTINUING EDUCATION – HOW TO MAKE IT WORK FOR YOU

Shaughnessy, Thomas W. Staff development in libraries: why it frequently doesn't take. *Journal of Library Administration*. 9(2): 5-12; 1988.

Technological advances, the desire of staff for professional advancement, the promise of increased job satisfaction and a commitment to improving user services are all factors which are spurring libraries to support continuing education for their staffs. But does it work, and if not, why not? The author describes what he sees as the basic elements of a successful staff development program. It must allow the staff member an opportunity for self assessment, it should involve structured team work, the program should take advantage of appropriate teaching methods and the most recent advances in learning theory, and it should take into account the goals of the organization of which the library is a part. Concern for staff development must be ongoing and involves a sustained commitment from the library administration. (KJP)

CBA IN LIBRARIES – CAN IT HELP?

Sridhar, M. S. Is cost benefit analysis applicable to journals use in special libraries? *The Serials Librarian*. 15(1/2): 137-153; 1988.

Cost-benefit analysis (CBA) is defined as ". . . the ratio of the benefits of a given project to its cost, taking into account the benefits and costs that cannot be directly measured in dollars." Library staff will often contend that, as a service organization, their activities are not susceptible to precise quantitative assessment; however, with fixed budgets and rising costs, there is a need to measure the benefit of services we offer. Although we do carry out cost-minimizing programs in such activities as weeding unused materials, economic factors are often not the most obvious considerations in these decisions. Several use studies are discussed, as well as the criteria used to determine value. A use study carried out at the Indian Space Research Organisation (ISRO) Satellite (ISAC) is described. Numbers of uses of 485 journals in their first three months on the shelf are compared to their subscription costs. Marginally used titles such as the *Journal of Applied Photographic Engineering* and *Telecommunication Journal of Australia* were suggested for cancellation. It was also recommended that 28 heavily used journals, used more than 30 times during the course of the study, be obtained by airmail or subscribed to in duplicate. As use is only one of several criteria applied to journals, it should not be the only criterion considered. However, when a title is perceived to be of high cost and low use, its retention must be considered most carefully. (KJP)

For Product Safety Concerns and Information please contact our EU representative GPSR@taylorandfrancis.com
Taylor & Francis Verlag GmbH, Kaufingerstraße 24, 80331 München, Germany

www.ingramcontent.com/pod-product-compliance
Lightning Source LLC
Chambersburg PA
CBHW052128300426
44116CB00010B/1822